GREATNESS

ALSO BY STEVEN F. HAYWARD

The Real Jimmy Carter

The Age of Reagan: The Fall of the Old Liberal Order, 1964–1980

Churchill on Leadership

GREATNESS

Reagan, Churchill, and the Making of

Extraordinary Leaders

Steven F. Hayward

THREE RIVERS PRESS

NEW YORK

Originally published in hardcover in the United States by Crown Forum, an
imprint of the Crown Publishing Group, a division of Random House, Inc.,
New York, in 2005.

Photograph on page 12 appears courtesy of the Ronald Reagan Library

Library of Congress Cataloging-in-Publication Data
Hayward, Steven F.
Greatness : Reagan, Churchill, and the making of extraordinary leaders /
Steven F. Hayward.
Includes bibliographical references and index.
1. Reagan, Ronald.   2. Churchill, Winston, Sir, 1874–1965.
3. Statesmen—United States—Biography.   4. Statesmen—Great
Britain—Biography.   5. Presidents—United States—Biography.   6. Prime
ministers—Great Britain—Biography.   7. United States—Politics and
government—1981–1989.   9. Political leadership—United States—Case
studies.   10. Political leadership—Great Britain—Case studies.   I. Title.
E877.H39 2005
941.084'092—dc22   2005007830

ISBN-13: 978-0-307-23719-4
ISBN-10: 0-307-23719-2

Printed in the United States of America

Design by Leonard Henderson

2 4 6 8 10 9 7 5 3 1

First Paperback Edition

To Norman and Winston,
and the future they will shape

CONTENTS

Great men are the ambassadors of Providence sent to reveal to their fellow men their unknown selves. . . . A wholesome regard for the memory of the great men of long ago is the best assurance to a people of a continuation of great men to come, who shall still be able to instruct, to lead, and to inspire.

—CALVIN COOLIDGE

GREATNESS

CHAPTER I

What Is Greatness?

*A democracy, not less than any other form of govern-
ment, needs great men to lead and inspire the people.*

— JAMES BRYCE, *The American Commonwealth*

RONALD REAGAN, like many American politicians of
both parties, liked to quote Winston Churchill.[1]
Reagan paraphrased him by name in his first presidential utterance, his inaugural address in 1981. "To paraphrase Winston Churchill," Reagan said, "I did not take the
oath I've just taken with the intention of presiding over the
dissolution of the world's strongest economy."[2] Reagan quoted
or mentioned the example of Churchill more than 150 times
during his presidency—more than three times as much as any
other president. Beyond the direct references, one finds that
Reagan discussed many political issues in the same terms, and
with the same vocabulary, as Churchill.

Many fine books have been written about Churchill and
Franklin Roosevelt, the contemporary world leaders and in-
dispensable partners of the Western alliance during World
War II. And the most apt Anglo-American comparison might

15

seem to be Churchill and the other Roosevelt—Theodore Roosevelt. Both were war heroes. Both were serious and accomplished writers and historians. Churchill certainly understood the meaning of TR's "bully pulpit" and his famous injunction to be "in the arena," getting your nose bloodied. In 1940 an American newspaper saw enough of the similarities to call Churchill "the Rough Rider of Downing Street." It turns out that TR, who met the young Churchill in 1900, didn't care for the brash young Englishman. His daughter, Alice Roosevelt Longworth, later told historian Arthur Schlesinger Jr. that her father disliked Churchill because "they were so much alike."

Meanwhile the affinity between Churchill and Reagan has been overlooked. Perhaps it is because, on the surface, Reagan and Churchill seem to be quite different people. Having written books about both men, however, I came to see that the comparison is a proper one, if for no other reason than the connecting thread of the Cold War. Churchill, with his famous Iron Curtain speech of 1946, made in the presence of Harry Truman, might be said to have launched the Cold War for the West. Reagan, a former Truman Democrat, ended it. Churchill said in the Iron Curtain speech that World War II could have been prevented "without the firing of a single shot." Reagan, heeding Churchill's vivid lesson, brought the Cold War to an end "without firing a single shot," Margaret Thatcher observed. (Indeed, Reagan's partnership with Thatcher in the 1980s could be seen as the very fulfillment of the Anglo-American unity that Churchill had envisioned in the Iron Curtain speech and elsewhere.)

As I began writing the second volume of my history of Ronald Reagan and his place in American political life (the forthcoming book *The Age of Reagan: Lion at the Gate, 1980–1989*), I recognized that the links between Reagan and Churchill extended beyond this Cold War connection. The parallels between the two men, I realized, were extensive, deep, and important. In particular, it became clear that pondering the cases of Churchill and Reagan side by side opens a window onto critical aspects of political genius, and political greatness, at the highest level.

That is why I have written this book. Unfortunately, the mainstream of contemporary history and political science does not adequately take account of the nature and sources of political greatness. Indeed, the egalitarian temper of modern intellectual life, combined with the reductionist methodology of social science, deprecates individual greatness and seeks to reduce the course of human affairs to material and subrational forces. Examining the lives and careers of Reagan and Churchill reminds us, however, that questions of how we understand political greatness deserve our attention.

What *is* greatness, especially political greatness? In three thousand years we have not surpassed the understanding of Aristotle, who summed up political greatness as the ability to translate wisdom into action on behalf of the public good. To be able to do this, Aristotle argued, requires a combination of moral virtue, practical wisdom, and public-spiritedness.[3] This is exceedingly problematic, as is evident from the difficulty Aristotle has explaining it. One must know not only what is good for oneself but also what is good for others. It is not enough merely to be wise or intelligent in the ordinary IQ-score sense; in fact, Aristotle goes to great lengths to show that practical wisdom "is at the opposite pole from intelligence." One must have moral virtue, judgment, and public spirit in a fine balance, and these traits must be equally matched to the particular circumstances of time and place.⁴ It is easy to go wrong, even with the best intentions.

Greatness is not an art or a science that can be mastered through standardized training. That is one reason why few are the people on whom we bestow the exalted title of *statesman*. But we can study examples of greatness, and learn to recognize it when it is in our midst.

The British historian Geoffrey Elton wrote, "When I meet a historian who cannot think that there have been great men, great men moreover in politics, I feel myself in the presence of a bad historian. And there are times when I incline to judge all historians by their opinion of Winston Churchill—whether they can see that, no matter how much better the details, often damaging, of the man and his career become known, he still remains, quite simply, a great man."⁵ Much the same thing can be said of Ronald Reagan.

CHAPTER 2

Parallel Lives I: Churchill and Reagan on the Surface

In politics a man, I take it, gets on not so much by what he does, as by what he is. It is not so much a question of brains as of character and originality.

—WINSTON CHURCHILL, 1897

WINSTON CHURCHILL and Ronald Reagan were not identical—no two people, not even twins, ever are. There were notable differences in their politics, personality, and intellect. For one thing, Churchill preferred Democrats to Republicans when it came to American politics, though he surely would have warmed to the ex-Democrat Reagan. Churchill was more enthusiastic about the welfare state than Reagan, supporting, for example, the creation of Britain's nationalized health insurance program, which was anathema to Reagan. Strictly measured by intellectual candlepower, Churchill had deeper perception of world affairs than Reagan.[1] But on the level of statecraft and achievement, they are more roughly equal. In some key insights, habits, character traits, and political practice, there are striking parallels.

On the surface this may seem a stretch; the two appear utterly dissimilar. Churchill was a lifelong statesman of the highest order, holding at some point in his fifty-year political career every important cabinet post except foreign secretary. He also wrote voluminous historical works, staking his claim to literary preeminence that culminated in the Nobel Prize for literature in 1953. Reagan is routinely dismissed as "just" an actor—a B-movie actor—most of his life, who took up politics as a second career in his mid-fifties. (In fact Reagan's political career should be dated from the late 1940s, when he became active in the highly charged political affairs of Hollywood.) Indeed, unlike Churchill, Reagan emphasized from the start that he was *not* a career politician. Yet even with his electoral success, Reagan continues to be dismissed as an uncurious, unintellectual lightweight.

But not so fast. Many of their dissimilarities begin to dissolve on closer inspection, and common aspects of their lives begin to dominate the comparison. For example, Churchill's friends and critics said to him on more than one occasion, "Winston—you missed your calling in life. *You should have been an actor!*" Churchill's political ally and friend David Lloyd George wrote in a letter in 1907 that Churchill "is just like an actor, he likes the limelight."[2] Churchill himself once compared his life to "an endless moving picture in which one was an actor," while President Reagan once referred to this aspect of Churchill's life, remarking in London in 1984, "Some say that if he wanted to, he could even have been a great character actor."[3]

A little-known fact about Churchill is that he did try his hand at screenwriting briefly in 1934, and he was also an early consultant on the film project that eventually became David Lean's *Lawrence of Arabia*.[4] In 1929 Churchill visited several

Hollywood film studios, where, as a guest of MGM, he struck up an acquaintance with Charlie Chaplin. Chaplin later visited him in England, and Churchill even proposed to write a screenplay for him, thinking he would be ideal for the role of the young Napoleon. When Churchill faced personal bankruptcy in the late 1930s, one of his ideas for restoring his finances was to quit politics and take up Hollywood screenwriting.[5] He sold the film rights to his autobiography, *My Early Life* (the resulting film, *Young Winston,* came out in 1972), and Cecil B. DeMille told Churchill that the script for *The Ten Commandments* had been inspired by Churchill's essay on Moses in *Thoughts and Adventures.*

Like Reagan, Churchill watched films frequently as a diversion from the stress of high office. He was fond of American westerns—Reagan's favorite genre—though it is not known whether Churchill ever saw any of Reagan's movies. Churchill is reported to have seen *That Hamilton Woman,* a 1941 film starring Lawrence Olivier and Vivien Leigh, seventeen times. Reagan commented to David Brinkley shortly before leaving the presidency in 1989, "I don't know how someone could do this job and *not* be an actor."[6] Like Reagan, Churchill understood the theatrical and dramatic aspects of political life.

Just as Churchill had some affinity for Reagan's original occupation, Reagan, we now know, had some of Churchill's literary inclinations. Reagan wrote short stories and poems in his youth. More recently it has been established that Reagan's mature literary output—long assumed to have been ghostwritten for him—came from his own hand in a quantity that is comparable to Churchill's prodigious output, albeit over a shorter time frame.

Churchill was more eloquent in the formal sense of the word; Reagan was more colloquial, as is the contemporary

American style of public speaking. (Harvey Mansfield Jr. commented wryly that Reagan was "as good a speaker as one can be without eloquence.") Churchill's speeches emphasized rhetorical flourishes and alliterative phrases. Reagan's style was plain and direct. Despite these formal differences in style, it is striking how alike Reagan and Churchill were in their approach to the task of public oratory. They used a similar format for their speech notes. Churchill wrote out detailed notes in a format that looked like free verse (or "psalm form," as one observer called it):

Steady continuous bombing,
     probably rising to great intensity
               occasionally,
       must be a regular condition of our life.

    The utmost importance preserve the morale of people,
       especially in the night work of factories.[7]

He also included stage directions to himself, such as "pause; grope for word," and "stammer; correct self."

Churchill's speech notes were prepared on four-by-eight sheets of paper, bound together through a hole punched in the corner. By the time he rose to speak, he had often spent twenty hours or more in preparation, and typically had the speech nearly memorized. The result, Churchill biographer William Manchester observed, was that Churchill's delivery "gives an illusion of spontaneity," making his speeches "a dramatic, vibrant occasion" in the House of Commons.[8]

Reagan also devoted extensive time preparing and refining his speeches. In the years before he reached the White House and began using a TelePrompTer, Reagan employed four-by-six cards (not three-by-five as the media misreported for years) for his shorthand speech notes, which he bound together with a rubber band. Reagan also included stage directions in parentheses ("pause for effect"). The result was similar to Churchill's delivery: Reagan's elaborate preparations made his speeches appear fluid and effortless. Martin Anderson, one of Reagan's closest policy advisers, notes that "Reagan's speech system gave the appearance of being casual and spontaneous, while in reality his speeches had the cold precision of any carefully researched and typed speech manuscript."[9] (A sample of one of Reagan's speech cards is displayed below.)

This methodical preparation carried over to other media. Reagan, as is now becoming better appreciated, was a consummate radio performer, giving more than a thousand radio

A speech card that President Reagan used for his remarks at the Lincoln Memorial on February 12, 1981. Reagan handwrote the text of the speech in the shorthand he had developed. *(Courtesy of the Ronald Reagan Library)*

addresses from 1975 to 1979 alone as he was preparing his successful run for the White House. Martin Anderson, Annelise Anderson, and Kiron Skinner have discovered 681 of Reagan's handwritten drafts of these radio addresses. Reagan probably wrote even more of his radio addresses, but the original drafts were lost or discarded. This corpus represents nearly a half-million words, comparable to an 800-page book. This is in addition to his estimated ten thousand personal letters.[10]

Churchill was also a practitioner of the radio address—not on the same scale as Reagan, but then there were fewer radio outlets available to him at the time. Churchill gave 148 radio addresses in the course of his political career, many of them the widely recalled speeches during wartime, which were mostly broadcasts of retaped speeches he had given in the House of Commons. (The House of Commons proceedings were not broadcast in those days.) BBC radio producer Grace Wyndham Goldie recalls, "Churchill took broadcasting seriously. He shaped each of his radio addresses with infinite care."[11] Beatrice Webb said of one of Churchill's early radio efforts, in 1926, that his performance was "a vividly rhetorical representation of his own case. . . . Except that his voice is harsh, he is a first rate broadcaster." The *Daily Express* newspaper noted that he achieved "extraordinary intimacy with his audience."[12]

The effect of their speeches is prominent among their claims to fame. Reagan was known as "the Great Communicator." Likewise Churchill is recalled for his stirring oratory; in Edward R. Murrow's memorable phrase, Churchill "mobilized the English language and sent it into battle." Robert Rhodes James offers a good summary of the powerful effect of Churchill's early wartime speeches:

It is often said that speeches do not affect votes in the House of commons; this is almost, though not quite, true. . . . What will always be remembered as the "blood, sweat and tears" speech was a real turning point. . . . It was Churchill's outstanding quality as a war leader that he had made the struggle seem not merely essential for national survival, but worthwhile and noble. No one—not even a child, as I was—who was in England in the summer of 1940 will ever forget the *cheerfulness* of the people. One caught Churchill's infectious spirit that this was a great time to be alive in; that Destiny had conferred a wonderful benefit upon us; and that these were thrilling days to live through.[13]

Churchill himself observed that in the summer of 1940 "there was a white glow, overpowering, sublime, which ran through our island from end to end."

Reagan was not up against the imminent destruction of the nation when he took office in 1981, though he did inherit an economic crisis, a national mood of pessimism, and fear that the nation had slipped into an irreversible decline. His rejection of the declinist mood, best exemplified in his predecessor Jimmy Carter's famous "crisis of confidence" (or "malaise") speech of 1979, was the real centerpiece of Reagan's 1980 campaign. He took direct aim at the view that "the United States has had its day in the sun, that our nation has passed its zenith. . . . My fellow citizens, I utterly reject that view." He returned to this again in his first moments in office. "We are too great a nation," Reagan said in his first inaugural address, "to limit ourselves to small dreams. We are not, as some would have us believe, doomed to an inevitable decline."

There was tangible evidence that people began to feel more optimistic under Reagan. A *New York Times*/CBS poll in the late summer of 1981 found a large swing toward optimism among Americans. Forty-six percent felt the nation would be better off by 1986, versus 29 percent who thought things could be worse. This was a sharp reversal from a previous *NYT*/CBS poll taken in 1979, when only 24 percent were optimistic about the future and 43 percent were pessimistic.

Beyond this morale boost, Reagan's speeches had decisive effects in the first year of his administration, when he was seeking to enact sweeping new economic policies. Throughout the spring and summer, it appeared that Reagan would not be able to get his budget plans and tax cuts through the Democratic-controlled House of Representatives. Three times Reagan went on national television to make his case and ask voters to write or call their congressmen to support his plan. Three times Reagan won the ensuing vote, after an overwhelming public response. The effectiveness of Reagan's television appeals was nearly unprecedented. Although it is common to think that every president enjoys the built-in advantage of the bully pulpit, academic studies have found surprisingly that nationwide presidential appeals usually have no effect or even a slight negative effect.[14] House Speaker Tip O'Neill admitted after Reagan's last speech, "We are experiencing a telephone blitz like this nation has never seen. It's had a devastating effect." An unnamed congressman told *Newsweek*, "I sure hope Reagan doesn't go on the tube again and say no more sex."

THE SIMILARITY IN their styles of preparing speeches, and the dramatic effect they had through their speeches, is only the beginning of a number of parallels and coincidences that run as a connecting thread between their very different lives. A comparison of Reagan and Churchill proceeds in three stages. It begins with the surface, with similarities that appear to be merely trivial or irrelevant to their politics. Second, their important differences must be understood. Perceiving their differences makes possible the ascent to the third stage, where the fundamental traits of statesmanship at the highest level emerge. The third stage of analysis reveals four common traits between Churchill and Reagan: imagination, insight, resoluteness, and independence of character and thought.

Among the coincidences that can be observed at the first stage of analysis is the fact that both men owed their initial political success to prior fame. Though Churchill was from a famous family, his exploits as a war hero in the Boer War catapulted him into the House of Commons after an initial failure. And Reagan obviously owed his initial success to having been a household name through his movie and television career. Many people achieve office on account of family, wealth, or celebrity background, however; staying and succeeding depend on something else. Churchill understood this early on, writing to his mother before his twenty-fifth birthday, "Introductions—connections—powerful friends—a name—good advice well followed—all these things count—but they lead only to a certain point. . . . Ultimately every man has to be weighed, and if found wanting nothing can procure him the public confidence."

Both men had a fondness for vigorous outdoor labor. In a startling similarity, they both dug fishponds of nearly identical dimensions at their country homes. Churchill built with his own hands a large brick wall at Chartwell, while Reagan built with his own hands long fences out of telephone poles at his ranch. (Reagan also hand-built a stone patio with rocks he rounded up on his ranch.) Clementine Churchill and Nancy Reagan disliked their husbands' country homes for the same reason: Chartwell and Rancho del Cielo were too remote from the bright lights and comforts of the metropolis. And both later came to appreciate them for the same reason: As their husbands ascended the political ladder, it was the one place where they could have some quiet privacy away from the crush of the political circus.

Both men nearly died of serious illness (pneumonia for Reagan in 1948 and a staph infection in 1981, and Churchill survived serious pneumonia several times) and both were nearly killed by violent trauma. Churchill was struck by a taxi on Fifth Avenue in New York in 1932; the impact threw him 30 feet in the air. As the world vividly recalls, Reagan was shot, whereupon one of his first statements upon awaking from surgery was to quote Churchill's famous line that "there is no more exhilarating feeling than being shot at without result," though this comment is not quite right, since this shot was not "without result." Churchill's personal courage is well known from his service in battle as a young man, and for his surprising decision to head off to the trenches in France to fight during World War I after being dismissed as First Lord of the Admiralty. Although Reagan was in the army in World War II, he never served in combat—his nearsightedness disqualified him—but the manner in which he faced his shooting gave proof of his courage. Senator Pat Moynihan, who was present in the White House on the day John F. Kennedy was killed in 1963, wrote a few days after Reagan's shooting, "In the history of the office has any man ever so triumphed over danger and pain and near death? We are surely proud of him." Even *The Nation* magazine, not ordinarily friendly to Reagan (to put it mildly), wrote, "His resilience provided a brief celebration of the tenacity of life and a reassuring glimpse at an appealing aspect of Ronald Reagan's character. . . . One half-expected to read upon awakening from the anesthesia he had quipped, 'Where's the rest of me?' "[15]

Among other odd coincidences and near coincidences, they both had artistic talent. Churchill took up painting during World War I and became a serious artist. Although Reagan never developed his artistic ability (his sketches and doodles show the germ of talent), as a young man he did briefly consider becoming a professional cartoonist. In the 1920s Churchill wrote an essay about what could be learned from cartoons. Both drew doodles and caricatures on their letters to their spouses.

As THE SUPERFICIAL coincidences accumulate, however, one begins to wonder whether their similarities reveal something deeper about their character that contributed to their political greatness. It is difficult to draw a bright line between mere coincidences and common aspects of their lives that point to some deeper source. Both men, for instance, switched parties, for nearly identical reasons. Both men acquired the reputation for being excitable adventurers with questionable judgment, if not outright warmongers. Yet nearly all their close associates gave a very different account of both men in times of crisis. "During crises [Reagan] tended to be quiet and even-tempered," reporter Lou Cannon wrote. "He was neither a war lover nor a demagogue."[16] Although Churchill was not immune to the effects of stress, having suffered two heart attacks and a serious bout of pneumonia during World War II, all his contemporaries testify to his calmness during times of crisis. One of Churchill's private secretaries, Eddie Marsh, observed in 1915, "The worse things go, the braver and serener he gets."[17]

The humor of both men is legendary; whole books have been filled with their quips and jokes. Alan Greenspan went as far as to say that Reagan was "psychologically a professional comedian, a professional raconteur." Churchill once said, "In my belief, you cannot deal with the most serious things in the world unless you also understand the most amusing." Cannon observed of Reagan, "He could laugh at himself because he knew he had a serious purpose."[18] Cannon points to a common trait of the humor of both men—self-deprecation. Again, examples are legion. When being questioned in the House of Commons during World War II about difficulties in the production of the new "Churchill" tank, Churchill explained, "This tank, the A22, was ordered off the drawing board, and large numbers went into production very quickly. As might be expected, it had many defects and teething troubles, and when these became apparent the tank was appropriately rechristened the 'Churchill.' These defects have now been largely overcome."[19] One can easily imagine Churchill's impish grin during the last sentence. In a 1987 speech Reagan related one of Churchill's more famous self-deprecating quips: "Winston Churchill was once asked, 'Doesn't it thrill you, Mr. Churchill, to know that every time you make a speech, the hall is packed to overflowing?' 'It's quite flattering,' Winston replied, 'but whenever I feel this way, I always remember that if instead of making a political speech I was being hanged, the crowd would be twice as big.' "

Robert Rhodes James observed that Churchill's humor, with some isolated exceptions, lacked cruelty and was most effective when he employed sarcasm. One of the most fondly recalled anecdotes has Churchill moving to the farthest urinal from Labour Party rival Clement Attlee in the men's room. Attlee jested that Churchill was being standoffish. Churchill explained his standoffishness with the ideologically tinted quip "Yes, whenever you see anything big you want to nationalize it." Sarcasm was also Reagan's strong suit. "A liberal's idea of being tough on crime"—to give just one Reagan example from the 1960s—"is to give out longer suspended sentences." Churchill had a close equivalent: "The Liberals' attitude [toward socialism] resembles a conversation which might take place between a band of hopeful missionaries and a band of cannibals while the cooking pot is actually being heated."

CHURCHILL IS TODAY a mythic figure, a larger-than-life statesman whom many argue was the greatest man of the twentieth century. Isaiah Berlin called Churchill "the largest human being of our time." *Time* magazine once thought so, too, naming him in 1950 "Man of the Half-Century." *(Time* drew away from this judgment in 2000, when it came time to designate the Person of the Century.) Although scholars still pick over Churchill's record and produce strong criticisms of him, the public generally overlooks or does not know of Churchill's weaknesses. Since his passing in June 2004, Reagan has also become a revered figure. Although many of the sharp judgments and criticisms routinely made of him are starting to fade, much of the common criticism of Reagan is still easily recalled.[20] Therefore it is astonishing to take a close look and note the number of contemporaneous judgments made about Churchill that sound exactly like many of the contemporaneous judgments about Reagan.

Reagan, it was often said, was out of touch with modern America, even oblivious to it. His plaid suits, if nothing else, were testimony to this, as were his taste in entertainment and his old-fashioned values. He openly championed the sexual modesty of the Hollywood of his heyday in the 1940s and 1950s against the permissiveness of the 1960s and 1970s. (When asked on *The Tonight Show* in 1972 if he might return to show business, Reagan replied, "Oh no, I'm much too old to take off all my clothes.") Churchill was similarly out of touch with contemporary moods. Isaiah Berlin observed that Churchill "created the mood and turned the fortunes of the Battle of Britain not by catching the mood of the country, but by being stubbornly impervious to it, as he had been to so many passing shades and tones of which the life around him has been composed."

Reagan was frequently criticized for ignoring facts or holding views contradicted by facts because he lived and thought in a world of "make-believe." Churchill would not necessarily have resisted this analysis as applied to himself. The young Churchill himself described his clearly autobiographical main character this way in his novel, *Savrola:* "Another world, a world more beautiful, a world of boundless possibility, enthralled his imagination." Jan Smuts said that Churchill's imagination "soared above the sober and often intransigent facts of reality." Churchill's physician, Lord Moran, wrote of "the inner world of make-believe in which Winston found reality," and psychiatrist Anthony Storr assessed Churchill in these terms:

> The kind of inspiration with which Churchill sus-
> tained the nation is not based on judgment, but on
> an irrational conviction independent of factual real-
> ity. Only a man convinced that he is on a heroic mis-
> sion, who believed that, in spite of all evidence to

the contrary, he could yet triumph, and who could identify himself with a nation's destiny could have conveyed his inspiration to others. The miracle had much in common with that achieved by a great actor, who, by his art, exalts us and convinces us that his passions are beyond the common run of human feeling. We do not know, and we shall never know, the details of Churchill's world of make-believe. But that it was there, and that he played an heroic part in it, cannot be gainsaid.[21]

Lou Cannon's assessment of Reagan tracks Storr's remarks on Churchill very closely:

Reagan already lived in a world of illusion before he arrived in Hollywood. . . . He used his optimistic imagination to transform his difficult childhood into an "idyll." . . . Later, he would invent an America that never was and share with his fellow citizens a bright, shining vision of our nation's greatness founded on an imagined version of the past. The vision would be accepted because of its power and because of Reagan's belief in it. But it was not a vision that thrives on close encounters.[22]

"Reagan's world of pretend," the *Washington Post*'s Haynes Johnson wrote, "led him to identify with superhuman heroes." And Garry Wills observed, "Nothing is more durable in Reagan than his dreams, his optimism, his religious-tinted hopes. Reagan does not argue for American values; he embodies them."[23]

What critical observers called Reagan's and Churchill's

penchant for a make-believe world abstracted from the cold facts is inextricably bound up with their extraordinary imagination. Far from being a weakness, this was perhaps the key source of *strength* for both men. In both cases there is a powerful historical dimension to their political imagination; each drew deeply on the historical sources of his nation's greatness, at a time when modern thought increasingly dismissed the past. Fashionable opinion deprecated both British imperialism and the American Founding at the time Churchill and Reagan were forming their mature political views, but they were unaffected. Only someone resolutely immune to fashionable opinion could be able to bend history to his will. Isaiah Berlin observed that "Churchill's political imagination has something of the same magical quality to transform [as Disraeli]." Berlin went on to extend this analysis to Franklin Roosevelt in a way that gives a strong insight into why Reagan remained a devotee of FDR even after switching parties: "Franklin Roosevelt, who as much as any man altered his country's inner image of itself and of its character and its history, possessed it in a high degree." This kind of imagination, Berlin pointed out, if filled with sufficient energy and force, "and, it may be added, fantasy, which is less frightened by the facts and creates ideal models in terms of which the facts are ordered in the mind, sometimes transforms the outlook of an entire people and generation."[24]

The peculiar imagination of both men manifested itself in small as well as large ways. It was Reagan's capacious imagination that led him to embrace missile defense, just as Churchill's imagination led him to champion a variety of military innovations (especially the tank). Then there was Reagan's fascination with "little green men," as Colin Powell called it. Reagan had been a science fiction fan during his acting career; the alter ego of Churchill's lone novel, *Savrola*, is diverted from politics by astronomy, "becoming each moment more under the power of the spell that star-gazing exercises on curious, inquiring humanity."[25] When Reagan met Gorbachev for the first time in 1985, he attempted to disarm him (so to speak) by saying that the differences between the United States and Soviet Union would instantly dissolve if the world faced invasion from aliens. It was a favorite theme that Reagan's aides worked to keep out of his public comments, but Reagan had his own mind. At the end of a speech to a high school audience shortly after the 1985 Geneva Summit, Reagan ad-libbed the theme (it is easy to tell from the fractured syntax that Reagan was departing from his written text):

> I couldn't help but—one point during our discussions privately with General Secretary Gorbachev—when you stop to think that we're all God's children, wherever we may live in the world I couldn't help but say to him, just think how easy his task and mine might be in these meetings that we held if suddenly there was a threat to this world from some other species, from another planet, outside the universe. We'd forget all the little local differences that we have between our countries, and we would find out once and for all that we really are all human beings here on this Earth together. Well, I don't suppose we can wait for some alien race to come down and threaten us, but I think that between us we can bring about that realization.[26]

Gorbachev had watched some old Reagan movies, and no doubt had read through the Soviet intelligence assessments of

Reagan that included prominently the fact that Reagan read his daily horoscope, in preparation for his first face-to-face meeting, but he was unprepared for this. Lou Cannon wryly notes that Gorbachev "did not have at his fingertips the Marxist-Leninist position on the propriety of cooperating with the imperialists against an interplanetary invasion," and promptly changed the subject.[27]

Among the most widespread criticisms of Reagan was that he was uninformed, even ignorant, and relied on simplistic platitudes to get by. "Reagan lacked a technical grasp of any issue, and he was usually bored by briefings," Cannon wrote. "To those who took a more traditional approach to the presidency, Reagan almost never seemed prepared."[28] Some of Churchill's top aides said the same thing. Field Marshal Alanbrooke, his top military aide during World War II, wrote in his dairy in 1944, "[Winston] has only half the picture in his mind, talks absurdities and makes my blood boil to listen to his nonsense."[29] George C. Marshall, Alanbrooke's American counterpart, agreed, saying, "His [Churchill's] planning was all wishing and guessing." In his personal diary President Eisenhower expressed frustration over Churchill's "almost childlike" views.

FOR ALL THEIR gregariousness, Reagan and Churchill were both remote, solitary men who lacked intimate friends. Despite Churchill's circle of admirers and supporters, such as fellow Conservative M.P. Brendan Bracken and "the Prof" Eric Lindemann, British historian J. R. Plumb noted that "friendship did not come easy to him." The same observation was made repeatedly about Reagan. Lou Cannon wrote that "Ronald Reagan was humanly accessible to people who had never met him and impenetrable to those who tried to know him well."[30] Haynes Johnson wrote, "At his core, there was something unknown or unknowable about Ronald Reagan."[31] Even Nancy Reagan has validated this view, telling Lou Cannon in 1989, "You can get just so far to Ronnie, and then something happens."[32] Their letters to their spouses also exhibit their solitary nature. Churchill wrote to Clementine in 1908, "I am a solitary creature in the midst of crowds."[33] Reagan wrote to Nancy from a film shoot in New York City in 1953, "Eight million people in this pigeon crap encrusted metropolis and suddenly I realized I was alone with my thoughts and they smelled sulphurous."[34]

Neither man showed much evidence of introspection. Storr thought "Churchill showed as little interest in the complexities of his own psychology as he did in the psychology of others."[35] C. P. Snow said Churchill's character was "abnormally impenetrable to most kinds of insight." Lou Cannon wrote of Reagan, "Reagan's inner life remained a mystery even to his friends."[36] PBS TV's Paul Duke said, "It's just impossible to get beyond the outer edges, to get him to be reflective or philosophical," while columnist George Anne Geyer complained that "Psychologically, I think he shuts out. . . . Reagan doesn't even begin to understand the forces at work in the world."[37] Reagan was regarded as a simple, straightforward person. For all of his brilliance, Churchill was much the same. J. R. Plumb wrote, "At the roots of his personality Churchill was a simple man as, I suspect, *most great statesmen are likely to be,* no matter how subtle and complex they may appear on the surface [emphasis added]."[38]

THEIR SIMILARITY ALSO extended to management philosophy, though less so to actual management practice. Churchill wrote that "those who are charged with the direction of supreme affairs must sit on the mountain tops of control; they must never descend into the valleys of direct physical and personal action." This was a noble lie in Churchill's case, as he was a notorious meddler and hound for details from subordinates far down the line. He admitted this to the House of Commons in 1942: "I am certainly not one of those who needs to be prodded. In fact, if anything, I am a prod."[39] Yet Churchill's is a good rule for the modern American presidency, which sits top a government so expansive that no president can realistically be expected to command it in detail.

Reagan's management style was typically described in one word: *delegation*. Reagan wrote in his autobiography, "I don't believe a chief executive should supervise every detail of what goes on in his organization. The chief executive should set broad policy goals and ground rules, tell people what he or she wants them to do, then let them do it; he should make himself (or herself) available, so that the members of his team can come to him if there is a problem."[40] Here it should be noted but deferred for full judgment elsewhere that Reagan's penchant for delegation and eschewing close oversight of details led to the one unmitigated disaster of his presidency, the Iran-Contra scandal.

While their stated management philosophies were the same, their executive styles were sharply different; in this way, they were nearly inverse images of each other, and the exact opposite of the standard in their respective countries. With his aggressive style, Churchill conducted himself more like an American president than a British prime minister, while Reagan's passive style was more like the normal practice of a British prime minister than a president. Churchill typically sought to dominate all meetings, usually spoke more than anyone else present, and pressed for firm decisions to be made at every meeting, if possible. Churchill's American-style traits were the source of much of the difficulty he experienced with his colleagues throughout his career.

Reagan was the opposite; he listened quietly as his aides would explain and argue among themselves. Occasionally he would interject a question or comment, but he usually kept his own counsel and reserved decisions until a later time. Churchill's description of Prime Minister Herbert Asquith could be applied to Reagan without amendment: "In Cabinet he was markedly silent. Indeed he never spoke a word in Council if he could get away without it. He sat, like the great judge he was, hearing with trained patience the case deployed on every side, now and then interjecting a question or brief comment, searching or pregnant, which gave matters a turn towards the goal he wished to reach; and when at the end, amid all the perplexities and cross-currents of ably and vehemently expressed opinion, he summed up, it was very rarely that the silence he had observed till then, did not fall on all."[41] It was precisely Asquith's passivity, Churchill later judged, that made him such a poor war leader after World War I began. Reagan's experience would be different.

THE SECOND LEVEL of a meaningful comparison of these two giants is to take an inventory of their important and obvious differences of temperament and character. As is well known, Churchill, like Abraham Lincoln, was prone to bouts of deep depression—what he called his "black dog." Reagan was a reliably optimistic and cheerful person—he had "a talent for happiness," George Will wrote—and was nearly incapable of being depressed. One should note, however, that despite his bouts of depression, Churchill maintained a willful philosophical optimism that was close to Reagan's. At the depths of the Munich crisis, in 1938, when Churchill delivered the greatest speech of his career, declaring that the Western democracies had been weighed in the balance and found wanting, Churchill wrote in a newspaper column, "It is a crime to despair. . . . It is the hour, not for despair, but for courage and rebuilding; and that is the spirit which should rule us in this hour."[42] "Never despair" was the concluding theme of his somber final speech as prime minister to the House of Commons in 1955.

Churchill was also slightly manic, a trait probably related to his depressive tendencies. No one would ever describe Reagan as manic. Churchill was legendary for his consumption of alcohol, though his drinking habits have been exaggerated, chiefly by Churchill himself. "I have taken more out of alcohol than alcohol has taken out of me," he liked to boast. Reagan, perhaps because of his father's severe alcoholism, was not much of drinker, preferring a weak gin blossom at the White House when the occasion called for cocktails.

Where Reagan was reserved, "Churchill's life was singularly lacking in inhibition or concealment," as biographer Roy Jenkins put it. "Of course I am an egotist," he admitted to a political rival. "Where do you get if you aren't?" The best expression of Churchill's enormous ego was his famous remark to Violet Bonham Carter when he was barely past thirty years old: "Curse ruthless time! Curse our mortality! How cruelly short is the allotted span for all we must cram into it! We are all worms. *But I do believe that I am a glow worm* [emphasis added]."[43] On another occasion Churchill rebutted his valet's complaint with the justification "But I am a great man."

Reagan would never have made either remark. His modesty was one of his most remarkable traits, an almost unheard-of quality among figures that reach the pinnacle of public life.

Churchill scholar Richard Langworth is undoubtedly correct that "President Reagan would deprecate being compared to the man he hailed as 'the pre-eminent statesman of [the twentieth] century.'"[44] Reagan's desktop slogan was an inversion of Harry Truman's "The Buck Stops Here." Reagan's motto was "There is no limit to what you can accomplish as long as you don't care who gets the credit." This modesty explains one huge gulf between Reagan and Churchill: Although Reagan was a proficient and prolific writer, he treated his obligatory postpresidential memoir with casual diffidence, turning over its production to a ghostwriter. No one would ever confuse the result, *An American Life*, with a masterpiece. Churchill, of course, was obsessed with writing his own place in history and produced several timeless masterpieces. As a colleague described Churchill's memoir of World War I, "Winston has written an enormous book about himself and called it *The World Crisis*," and Arthur Balfour called the book "an autobiography disguised as a history of the universe."[45]

Of course, Reagan was secure enough to know that he would get the credit (or blame) for events whether he deserved it or not, but it is still passing strange that this remote and nonintimate person would be so quick to share credit with others. A good example is the way Reagan used to talk about his time as governor of California, which he represented as a key qualification to become president in 1980. In describing his record, he almost invariably used the pronoun *we* instead of *I*. Reagan explained in a letter, "I use the plural 'we' because, as governor I had the help of some very fine people."[46] His future wife Nancy Davis noted when she met him in 1949 that "he didn't talk about himself; he didn't talk about his movies. He talked about a lot of things, but not about 'my next picture, my last picture.'"[47]

This brings us to the always necessary but troublesome political quality of ambition. The ambition of the two men appears very different at first sight. Churchill's ambition was always obvious; he readily admitted to it, and always reached for justifications. "The one real difficulty I have to encounter," Churchill wrote 1902, "is the suspicion that I am moved by mere restless ambition." He was right. Sir Charles Dilke, who had written that Lord Rosebery was the most ambitious man he had ever known, later amended this judgment: "I have since known Winston Churchill." After Churchill switched parties for the first time in 1904, his former Tory partisans attacked him as "a political adventurer who would do anything for his own advancement."

Reagan's ambition was no less intense than Churchill's but was always muted or concealed. Reagan's outward modesty may have been more a matter of calculation than we will ever be able to unravel, because not only was it authentically rooted in his character, it also was a principal means of veiling his ambition. First in Hollywood and then in politics, Reagan always carried on as if his ascent were of the greatest of ease, even though we know behind the scenes he was careful and deliberate. The next chapter will speculate on some of the reasons Reagan affected his easygoing manner even as he was burning with ambition. For now, it is enough to record that his ambition is discernible only if one looks closely. A good example is his penchant for brown suits. Brown suits are the regular man's suit in most of the country, in contrast to the dark colors and pinstripes that are the fashion of the elite. All of Reagan's suits—and shirts—were hand-tailored, but on camera he appears quite ordinary, which is exactly the image he wanted to project. Here and there are subtle hints of Reagan's hidden vanity. In his diary entries, for example, he made care-

ful note of how many times a speech was interrupted with applause—something that also obsessed the insecure megalo-
maniac Lyndon Johnson. Another telling fact is the way
Reagan picked himself up at several points when his entertainment career stalled out, and created something new when
others might have given up. Reagan essentially reinvented
himself several times. The same trait showed itself in politics.
Just about everyone, including his inner circle of political advisers, thought he was done with politics after his close loss to
Gerald Ford in 1976—everyone but Reagan himself.

SURVEYING THE SIMILARITIES and differences between the
two statesmen brings us to the third and decisive level of
analysis, which is their quality of mind. This is revealed in
their imagination and insight into the times in which they
lived, and their independence from the conventional wisdom
of even their own political parties. Abraham Lincoln wrote
that all nations have a *central* idea, from which all its minor
thoughts radiate. The same can be said of great statesmen.
Churchill's central insight might be said to be that the distinction between liberty and tyranny is real and substantial. The
perception may seem trivial or obvious, until we stop to realize
that modern "value-free" social science has gone very far in ef-
facing the moral distinctions between different kinds of
"regimes" (as political scientists say). This blurring of the
edges has a long pedigree: Thomas Hobbes wrote in *The
Leviathan* that tyranny is merely "kingship misliked," and one
will scour modern political science textbooks in vain to find
the Soviet Union described as a "tyranny," though it is one of
the oldest categories of rule known to political thought.

If the distinction between liberty and tyranny is real and
substantial, it follows that compromise with tyrannical evil is

not possible. Almost everyone agrees, which is why the desire
for accommodation must begin by denying or obfuscating evil
and tyranny. It was precisely this instinct for evasion that lay
behind the furious reaction against Churchill's anti-Nazi
speeches of the 1930s, and against Reagan's "evil empire"
speech of 1983. Churchill warned of the nature of Nazism
starting as early as 1930, three years before Hitler came to office, and as his warnings increased along with the growing
menace, he was met mostly with antagonism from his own
party, chiefly because he laid out the problem with a clarity
and with a call for choice and action that most hoped to avoid
through wishful thinking. At root, Churchill understood and
took seriously that Hitler meant what he had written in *Mein
Kampf,* a book few Britons had bothered to read and would
not have taken seriously if they had. Likewise Reagan understood and took seriously the resolve of Lenin and his successors, quoting often Lenin's statement "It is inconceivable that
the Soviet Republic should continue to exist for a long period
side by side with imperialistic states. Ultimately, one or the
other must conquer."

Reagan's central idea was a variation of Churchill's, and
can be summarized as the view that unlimited government is
inimical to liberty, in its vicious forms, such as Communism or
socialism, but also in its supposedly benign forms, such as bureaucracy. Reagan expressed his broad view of the problem in
his 1982 speech to the British Parliament: "There is a threat
posed to human freedom by the enormous power of the modern state. History teaches the danger of government that over-
reaches: political control takes precedence over free economic
growth; secret police, mindless bureaucracy—all combining to
stifle individual excellence and personal freedom." Reagan's

conflation here of "secret police" and "mindless bureaucracy" shows the harmony of purpose in his own mind between his domestic and foreign policies—shows that the problem of government power was for him not a dichotomy between East and West but a philosophical and practical continuum.[48]

The combination of imagination, independence, and insight is manifested finally in a high degree of resoluteness, which can easily be confused with unyielding stubbornness. There are countless examples of the stubbornness of both men against the advice and consensus of their political circle. This stubbornness was an essential asset to both men, even in cases where it seemed foolhardy or counterproductive. One might point to Reagan's opposition in 1977 to the Panama Canal treaties, which transferred U.S. sovereignty of the American-built canal to Panama, as roughly analogous to Churchill's vehement and unpopular opposition to granting dominion status to India in the 1930s. In both cases Reagan and Churchill split their own parties and lost the immediate legislative battle. In both cases, however, it was a defeat with positive consequences.

Reagan's great political ally William F. Buckley Jr. tried to convince him to support the Panama Canal treaty, and later argued that Reagan was lucky to have lost the fight over the treaty, for the simple reason that rejection of the treaty might have led to a violent confrontation with Panama, for which Reagan would have been blamed. It is doubtful, Buckley believed, that Reagan would have survived the episode to become president in 1980. Reagan's previous stubbornness over the Panama Canal gave weight to his policy toward Latin America during his presidency. A decade later, when turmoil in Panama led to an American military intervention under the first President Bush, a number of earlier supporters of the Panama Canal treaties expressed some public doubts about whether they had been right.

Churchill's seemingly unreasonable stubbornness over India ironically became a source of reassurance for the nation when war came. Harry Jaffa explains, "And so Churchill's willfulness, his stubbornness, his refusal to take counsel against his own sense of the fitness of things—his preference, so to speak, to being shamed before the world rather than be ashamed of himself—in the end served him better than he knew, or than he could have known. By 1940 he was the only man the country would trust to see it through."[49]

The nature and sources of their common traits will be explored in more detail in the next several chapters; for the moment, it is useful to observe that the same criticism was once made of both men—that they were relics of the past, with dangerous or reckless views, not to be trusted with high office. Isaiah Berlin wrote that "Churchill remains a European of the nineteenth century," and the Socialist intellectual Harold Laski called Churchill "one of the great anachronisms of our time . . . a gallant and romantic relic of 18th century imperialism."[50] In Reagan's case, even some of his top aides, such as David Stockman, long regarded him as "primitive." Reagan, it was joked, should go back to making movies for Eighteenth Century Fox.

In both cases, after their subsequent leadership ability and political success became undeniable, this criticism was turned on its head and became the explanation of their success. Churchill's old-fashioned, Victorian-era British-bulldog-cum-Manichaeanism was exactly what was necessary to confront Hitler in 1940; Reagan's old-fashioned, sentimental

Americanism and optimism were exactly suited to the moment of national self-doubt at the end of the 1970s.

The explanation is wrong in both cases, as this book will argue. There is something else besides fidelity to the past that explains why we have long considered the case of Churchill to be extraordinary, and increasingly why we are beginning to regard Ronald Reagan in the same class. There are lessons here for students of politics and history that are applicable to the new and difficult challenges of our own time. Perhaps the similarity of their statecraft offers lessons for the leaders of the twenty-first century.

So how did these outwardly dissimilar men come to be so alike in decisive respects, and come to play such important roles on the world stage? Let us begin at the beginning.

CHAPTER 3

Parallel Lives II: From Childhood to Maturity

So on the grounds that this man [Cyrus] was worthy of wonder, we examined who he was by birth, what his nature was, and with what education he was brought up, such that he so excelled in ruling human beings. Whatever we have learned, therefore, and think we have perceived about him, we shall try to relate.

— XENOPHON, *The Education of Cyrus*

ONE WAY of appreciating the similarities and differences between Ronald Reagan and Winston Churchill is to compare their early autobiographies side by side. In 1930 Churchill published *My Early Life: A Roving Commission*, covering his life story through the year 1908, when he was thirty-four; in 1965 Reagan published *Where's the Rest of Me?*, covering his life story up to age fifty-four, the point when he decided to enter politics as a candidate for California governor. Both later published additional memoirs after their times in high office, but as a window into the formative years of their lives, *My Early Life* and *Where's the Rest of Me?* are the best two books to consult.

On the surface their childhoods and early upbringing appear worlds apart. Churchill was born in one of Britain's largest country homes, to illustrious parents ensconced in the aristocracy, which assured Winston a place at the top of Britain's class-oriented social structure. In fact, Churchill's birth made national news. Reagan was born to modest circumstances. "Later in life," Reagan wrote in his memoirs, "I learned that, compared with some of the folks who lived in Dixon, our family was 'poor.' But I didn't know that when I was growing up. And I never thought of our family as disadvantaged."[1] The Reagan household was in fact a downwardly mobile family; each successive house they rented in their nearly annual moves was worth less, according to tax-assessment records, than their previous home.[2] And this was before the onset of the Great Depression.

But after one gets beyond the differences in their social and material circumstances, common aspects begin to emerge. Reagan and Churchill both had the circumstances of a potentially unhappy childhood. Yet while both record in their memoirs scenes of heartrending sadness from their childhoods, neither man regarded his early years as unhappy.[3] Quite the opposite; it is notable that these first memoirs of the early lives of both men are self-deprecating accounts that recall their childhoods with fondness and alacrity. Possibly this reflects a willful determination on the part of each man, rooted in their ambitious characters and large souls, to surmount the unhappiness of their childhood by transforming it in their own minds, thereby developing their powerful imaginations, the central pillars of their political genius.

In typical American fashion, Reagan recalls much of his early childhood as a "Huck Finn–Tom Sawyer idyll." While Churchill writes of hating his first boarding school, he writes about the experience with an ironic wit that suggests he knows the experience was good for him, or at the very least suggests an innate reservoir of optimism, like Reagan's, that made the experience productive. In fact their childhood circumstances probably contributed to their ambition. Psychiatrist Anthony Storr thought so in Churchill's case, offering an analysis that may apply equally to Reagan: "Ambition, when as in Churchill's case it is a compulsive drive, is the direct result of early deprivation. For if a child has but little inner conviction of his own value, he will be drawn to seek the recognition and acclaim which accrue from external achievement."[4]

Both boys had a fondness for sports, especially swimming, and both were fascinated with toy soldiers, which only marks them out as being normal little boys. But both noted this interest in their memoirs. Reagan: "In Chicago I got a serious case of bronchial pneumonia and while I was recuperating one of our neighbors brought me several of his son's lead soldiers. [This is yet another coincidence; Churchill nearly died of pneumonia as a young boy.] I spent hours standing them up on the bed covers and pushing them back and forth in mock combat. To this day I get a little thrill out of seeing a cabinet full of toy soldiers."[5] Churchill had an extensive collection of more than a thousand toy soldiers, to which he later attributed his interest in taking up a military career in early adulthood. "This orientation was entirely due to my collection of soldiers," he wrote; "the toy soldiers turned the current of my life."[6]

Churchill's parents kept a studied distance from him, as was typical of British aristocracy in those days (though some biographers suggest that Churchill's father actively disliked him). "The neglect and lack of interest in him shown by his parents were remarkable," Churchill's son Randolph wrote, "even judged by the standards of the late Victorian and Edwardian days." The British upper class coined the old saying that children should be seen and not heard; Churchill's parents amended this to include that children should be neither seen nor heard. He was shuttled off to a series of boarding schools starting at the age of eight, where he was an unhappy student, grieving at his remoteness—physically and emotionally—from his parents. Even when Winston was at home, he was in the care and supervision of a governess rather than his parents. Reagan's childhood family life was more normal, except that his father's intermittent alcoholism drew a veil between him and the rest of his family.

BOTH MEN HAD awkward relationships with their fathers; in Reagan's case, because of his father's drinking; in Churchill's case, because he was physically away from his father for most of his childhood and early adulthood. And Jack Reagan's alcoholism finds a rough parallel in Churchill's father's illness (thought to be either syphilis or a brain tumor), which degenerated into dementia and ultimately took his life at the age of forty-four. Despite this distance, Reagan and Churchill idolized their fathers, and one can tell from their descriptions of their fathers' characters something of why Reagan and Churchill turned out as they did. ("What a strange thing heredity is," Churchill once wrote in a letter. "We are really only variants of what has gone before.")

Ronald Reagan became noted in adulthood for his humor and storytelling skills. He was emulating his father, of whom Reagan wrote, "He was the best raconteur I ever heard, especially when it came to the smoking-car sort of stories."[7] Reagan described his father as "a restless man, burning with ambition to succeed." Winston said the same thing about his father, whose stellar career came to an abrupt crash in 1886 in an act of political self-immolation. (Randolph Churchill, serving as chancellor of the exchequer, had abruptly resigned, thinking he could bring down Prime Minister Salisbury and take the office for himself. The strategy failed, ending Randolph's career in high office.) Churchill venerated his father's political career and especially his justly renowned oratorical skills. Churchill wrote that "he seemed to own the key to everything or almost everything worth having." Churchill studied and memorized his father's speeches, and longed for comradeship with this father, once offering in early adulthood to serve as his father's private secretary. To all of these entreaties Randolph Churchill "was immediately offended" and "froze me into stone."[8] Winston's dearest childhood hope that he could take to his father's side on the floor of the House of Commons as a fellow MP was foreclosed by Randolph's early death in 1895, a few days after Winston's twenty-first birthday.

The pain of the rejection and distance between Winston and his diseased father finds its analogue in Reagan's oft-recalled experience at age eleven of finding his drunken father passed out in the snow in front of their house. With his arms outstretched, Jack Reagan appeared to Ronald as though he were crucified. Although Ronald Reagan wrote that he "could feel no resentment against him," Jack Reagan's place in Ronald Reagan's life noticeably receded after this episode. Henceforth and throughout the rest of his life, it was Reagan's mother that dominated his memory and thoughts. Churchill overlooked his father's disdain and decrepitude, recalling his father in his maiden speech in the House of Commons in 1901 as "a certain splendid memory." Reagan was less successful putting his father's "demons" out of his mind, but he also chose to emphasize "the bluff, hearty man I knew and loved and will always remember."

While both men acquired decisive traits from their fathers, it was to their mothers that they owed their deepest feelings of affection and guidance. "My mother always seemed to me a fairy princess: a radiant being possessed of limitless riches and power," Churchill wrote of his mother, Jennie. "She shone for me like the Evening Star."[9] Reagan's mother, Nelle, was a devout evangelical Christian, from whom Reagan acquired much of his native optimism and sense of Providence—both for himself personally and for America. "I have heard from more than one psychiatrist," Reagan wrote on the first page of *Where's the Rest of Me?*, "that we imbibe our ideals from our mother's milk. Then, I must say, my breast feeding was the home of the brave baby and the free bosom."[10] From his mother, Reagan testified throughout his life, he acquired the belief that God has a plan for each one of us. In a personal letter, Reagan wrote of his mother's influence, "I now seem to have her faith that there is a divine plan, and while we may not be able to see the reason for something at the time, things do happen for a reason and for the best. One day what has seemed to be an unbearable blow is revealed as having marked a turning point or a start leading to something worthwhile." (The religious views of Reagan and Churchill will be considered more fully in Chapter 5.)

ANOTHER PARALLEL BETWEEN Reagan and Churchill is that both had early adult loves that lasted for several years, appeared headed for marriage, but then ended abruptly and sadly. Reagan's first adult love was Margaret Cleaver, the daughter of the pastor of his church in Dixon. "For almost six

years of my life I was sure she was going to be my wife,"
Reagan wrote. "I was very much in love." Reagan even gave her
an engagement ring. Then, while Reagan was working at his
first radio job in Iowa and Cleaver was working as a school-
teacher in Illinois, she fell in love with a foreign service officer
while on a European cruise, and returned—by mail—the engagement ring to Reagan. He was shattered.

Churchill's first love was Pamela Plowden, whom he met
in India in 1896. It was love at first sight: "I must say that she is
the most beautiful girl I have ever seen," Churchill wrote to
his mother. Churchill and Plowden corresponded faithfully
over the next several years as Churchill continued his ambitious travels as a military correspondent. Plowden tired of
waiting, and after five years of dropping hints that Churchill
should propose, became engaged to the Earl of Lytton. In
both cases Reagan and Churchill let their first loves get away
because they felt themselves not well enough established, pro-
fessionally and financially, to wed.

Reagan later married Hollywood starlet Jane Wyman.
Churchill wanted to marry a starlet; he proposed to Ethel
Barrymore in 1902, but she turned him down on the grounds
that she was not cut out for the world of politics. (They remained acquaintances: Churchill sent Barrymore a congratu-
latory telegram on the occasion of her eightieth birthday.)
Churchill finally settled on Clementine Hozier, marrying her
in 1908 and, as he put it in the last sentence of *My Early Life*,
"lived happily ever afterward." Reagan had his own matrimo-
nial version of "lived happily ever afterward." Countless times
he would tell dinner guests and audiences, "And then along
came Nancy Davis and saved my soul."

Reagan's second marriage to Nancy Davis resembles in
many ways Churchill's marriage to Clementine. Nancy, like

Clementine, became Reagan's political partner. As Churchill's daughter Mary (now Lady Soames) puts it, "Clementine possessed that most important ingredient in a politician's make-up—a good political instinct. She was also, on the whole, a better judge of people than Winston. She did not approve of, or like, several of his friends."[11] Nancy Reagan played a similar role for Ronald, frequently being the instigator of staff changes that Ronald would have resisted left to himself. On the other hand, both spouses were unenthusiastic about many aspects of party politics. Clementine tried to talk Winston out of becoming the formal leader of the Conservative Party following the death of Neville Chamberlain in November 1940, and Nancy Reagan privately disdained many of the "movement conservatives" who formed the core of Ronald Reagan's political base.

At Churchill's wedding, Dean Weldon, previously his schoolmaster at Harrow and then the Bishop of Manchester, said, "There must be in the stateman's life many times when he depends upon the love, the insight, the penetrating sympathy and devotion of his wife. The influence which the wives of our statesmen have exercised for good upon their husbands' lives is an unwritten chapter of English history."[12] Churchill's son Randolph wrote that Winston's marriage to Clementine "proved the sheet anchor of his career. . . . Throughout the convulsions of political life and the waging of the two greatest wars in history, their love remained constant and abiding. As Churchill often remarked in other contexts, 'Here firm, though all be drifting.' "[13] Change "Clementine" to "Nancy" in these passages and you have the exact description of the Reagans' marriage.

Yet the relationship between Winston and Clementine, and that between Ronald and Nancy, was not a coldly calculating union. At its core was a romantic love of almost adolescent sentimentality that comes across in their personal letters. Winston and Clementine, both fond of animals (the Churchills kept a veritable menagerie at Chartwell), had animal nicknames for each other: Winston was "pug," and Clementine "kat" or "Clemmie-Kat." They would oink and meow at each other. Typical salutations in their personal letters included, "Goodbye my little Puggie Wow," signed, "Clemmie Kat."[14] Winston would draw a picture of a pug at the bottom of his letters, which would close on notes such as "I love you so much & it grieves me to feel you are lonely."[15]

Reagan called Nancy "Nancy-pants," and would send her sentimental love notes from movie sets and, later, from the Oval Office. Reagan would occasionally draw a likeness of his face, sad and tearful at the absence of Nancy ("Look what happens when I'm without you," read one message). Typical is Reagan's handwritten letter on White House stationery, March 4, 1981: "Dear First Lady: As Pres. of the United States it is my honor and privilege to cite you for your service above and beyond the call of duty in that you have made one man (me) the most happy man in the world for 29 years. . . . She has done this in spite of the fact that he still can't find the words to tell her how lost he would be without her."

While their marriages were extraordinarily close, both men had awkward and difficult relationships with their children. Churchill arguably overcompensated with his children for the distance his own parents had kept from him. It didn't work. Churchill's son Randolph was a frequent embarrassment, both politically and otherwise. Randolph's attempts to emulate his father's political success by running for Parliament were mostly unsuccessful, and often caused difficulties with Conservative Party leaders. Reagan's daughter

Maureen similarly attempted to parlay the family name into a U.S. Senate seat in California in 1982, but Reagan stayed scrupulously neutral, dooming her chances. Churchill had to settle Randolph's debts on several occasions, and endured press accounts of Randolph's drunkenness and rude behavior. (Randolph's irascible reputation prompted one of Evelyn Waugh's best put-downs. When Randolph had a benign tumor removed, Waugh commented, "Typical of modern science to find the one bit of Randolph Churchill that is not malignant, and remove it.") Sarah Churchill, Winston's second daughter, insisted on marrying an older, twice-divorced music hall co-median, Vic Oliver, over Winston and Clementine's strong objections. Sarah eloped with Oliver to New York to marry. They predictably divorced; Sarah was married twice more.

Reagan's son Ronald dropped out of Yale, over his par-ents' objections, to take up ballet dancing, where he was a modest success. He decided to marry a fellow dancer, Doria Palmieri, whom he had met in New York. He gave his mother and father just twenty-four hours notice that the wedding would take place. Patti Davis, Reagan's other child with Nancy, so distanced herself from her parents that she adopted her mother's maiden name. She also adopted the leftist politics of her father's opponents, appearing at anti-Reagan rallies and political events throughout much of his presidency, and keep-ing company with rock musicians and other celebrities who landed her regularly in the gossip columns. (Ron also repudi-ated his father's political views, though in a more subdued fashion.) All of Reagan's children, except Ron, wrote memoirs that dwelt to varying degrees on the family's dysfunctions.

The passage of time brought a measure of reconciliation to both families. Some latitude must be given to the children of famous and prominent people. It cannot have been easy to be the child of Churchill or Reagan, and it is not unusual to find family strain in such circumstances. *The Weekly Standard*'s Noemie Emery observed, "It is no accident that the presidents whose children showed the most overt hostility were those of Ronald Reagan and Franklin Roosevelt, two great national leaders who found it much easier to establish the illusion of intimacy with millions of strangers than to establish the real thing with their children."[16]

THESE SIMILARITIES IN their upbringing and personal lives can be marked off as superficial, though at some point basic laws of probability would suggest that so many similarities are beyond mere coincidence. Regardless of the nature of the likenesses described here, they are mostly secondary to their politics. A closer look shows that their education was central to the evolution of their political similarities. But their formal education was not their *real* education, at least as far as politics is concerned. Their real education is the subject of the next chapter.

CHAPTER 4

The Education of Statesmen

*The reader must remember that not having been to a
university, I had not been through any of those processes
of youthful discussion by which opinion may be formed
or reformed in happy irresponsibility.*

—WINSTON CHURCHILL, *My Early Life*

*I let football and other extracurricular activities eat into
my study time with the result that my grade average was
closer to the C level required for eligibility than it was to
straight A's. And even now I wonder what I might have
accomplished if I'd studied harder.*

—RONALD REAGAN,
EUREKA COLLEGE, 1982

CAN POLITICAL greatness—the genius of the statesman—be taught? Churchill didn't think so.[1] "Genius,"
he wrote in his biography of his great ancestor John
Churchill, the first Duke of Marlborough, "cannot be acquired, either by reading or experience." This is an especially
apt question in an age when "leadership studies" are all the

61

rage. Are the great figures among us born that way, pure flukes in some indescribable way? Churchill plainly was born to politics, in typical British fashion. American political culture is very different. With a few important exceptions, such as the Adams, Roosevelt, Kennedy, and Bush families, America's leaders tend to arise from the ranks of ordinary and often lowly rank: Lincoln, Truman, Nixon, Carter, Clinton—and Reagan.

It is surely true that political genius cannot be taught in the same fashion as mathematics, law, or medicine. Otherwise supreme examples of political greatness—those individuals we laud as "statesmen"—would be more common. That they are not more common is testimony both to the inherent difficulty of politics and the limitations of human character. In explaining the political greatness of Churchill and Reagan, one must answer a fundamental question: Why were they unique among their contemporaries, most of whom shared the same upbringing and formal education, and often the same general views about key issues? Explaining Reagan and Churchill as products of their environment or historical context is clearly incorrect. In the end what was decisive about Churchill and Reagan was their informal *self*-education. Both were political autodidacts. Combined with the example of the self-taught Abraham Lincoln, who could be considered America's first home-schooled president, one wonders whether self-education might be a marker for great statesmen.

Certainly their formal education does not provide the key to their political insight. An identical myth surrounds both Reagan's and Churchill's childhood—that they were poor students. In Churchill's case, he is the author of this myth, deprecating his skill at Latin, Greek, mathematics, and other subjects that bored him. Churchill writes that he "enjoyed few gleams of success" in school. "I was on the whole considerably discouraged by my school days. . . . In retrospect these years form not only the least agreeable, but the only barren and unhappy period of my life."[2] To be sure, Churchill ranked near or sometimes at the bottom of his class in his early years in school (he also received bad marks for behavior—an early sign of his rebellion against authority), but it should be recalled that he was enrolled in elite boarding schools that had stiff prerequisites for entry, a fact Churchill skips over in his memoir. Finishing low (as opposed to failing) in these schools would be like saying a low finisher in the Olympic marathon is a bad runner: in both cases, you have to be very good to make the field in the first place.

It is clear Churchill's problem in school was boredom rather than dullness or slowness. As he put it, "Where my reason, imagination or interest were not engaged, I would not or could not learn." A close reading of Churchill's account of his education in *My Early Life* reveals the precociousness and early signs of brilliance that would become obvious later in his life. Churchill thrilled to the infrequent lectures about large subjects and thought they should have been a primary means of instruction (as, indeed, they are in higher education). Students should write reflective essays on the lectures, "then the masters would soon begin to find out who could pick things up as they went along and make them into something new, and who were the dullards; and the classes at school would soon get sorted out accordingly." Churchill desired an education that employed thinking skills. Such a method, Churchill concludes in a revealing phrase, "would not have stultified itself by keeping me at the bottom of the school."[3] As it was, the young Churchill not surprisingly excelled in history and English, even as he performed poorly in most other subjects.

Reagan's trouble with school was the opposite of Churchill's. Reagan showed early signs of high intelligence, and was a well-behaved pupil. He began reading on his own at the unusually early age of four. Reagan did very well in his first years of elementary school, earning top marks in math and spelling in the first and second grades. But after these first few years, he settled into the ranks of average students. He became known, especially at Eureka College, as a C- student, which contributed significantly to his later reputation as an intellectual lightweight. Like Churchill, Reagan always recalled his formal education with insouciance. His college record prompted one of Reagan's favorite quips as president: "I often wondered how far I might have gotten in life if I had studied harder."

We can only speculate about the reasons for Reagan's reversion to the mean, but one plausible hypothesis is that the family's constant movement — Reagan was in a different elementary school for his first three grades, because his father's difficulty holding a job compelled the family to move almost every year — combined with the shame of his father's alcoholism, contributed to the slight shyness and personal distance that became one of Reagan's most pronounced character traits later in life. The smartest kid in the class is seldom the most popular kid in the class. Reagan would later write openly, but with few details, about his childhood insecurities and lack of self-confidence. Michael Barone and Martin Anderson both theorize that Reagan figured out early in life that the best way to adjust to his unstable circumstances was to eschew being the smart kid. This would fit with Reagan's later persona as the "hale fellow well met."

During these early years Reagan and Churchill both displayed a trait that was instrumental to their later careers: both men had a near-photographic memory, combined with an inclination toward public performance. Reagan's mother was an amateur thespian who organized small-scale dramatic readings and plays in the community. Nelle Reagan persuaded Ronald to try out memorizing a speech and giving it in front of a small audience when he was about twelve years old. Overcoming his shyness and insecurity, he gave the speech and discovered the thrill of audience applause and appreciation. It was the beginning of Reagan's fascination with public drama.

Churchill's phenomenal memory and inclination toward public speaking—despite a mild lisp and a slight stutter—also exhibited themselves at an early age, when he memorized and recited without error 1,200 lines of Macaulay's "Lays of Ancient Rome," thereby taking first prize at the Harrow School competition. Churchill could still recite long passages from memory more than sixty years later, along with poems he had read decades before in *Punch* and other popular magazines. Once something was in Churchill's head it was there for good.

Churchill's innate intelligence finally exhibited itself in conventional form at the next stage of his education, at Sandhurst, Britain's equivalent to West Point. Though Churchill struggled to pass the entrance exam (it required a special tutor and three tries at the test), he ranked near the top of his class now that he was studying subjects that absorbed his imagination (tactics, fortification, topography, military law and administration, and so forth). No longer was he arranging toy soldiers on a board; now he was doing the real thing. His performance at Sandhurst "shows that I could learn quickly enough the things that mattered."

He was thrilled to have been placed in the track to become a cavalry rather than an infantry officer, because this meant he could work on his horsemanship. "What fun it would be having a horse!" Churchill wrote. (His father, who had to pay for the horse and its upkeep, was less thrilled.) Reagan joined the U.S. Army's Fourteenth Cavalry Regiment as a reservist during his radio days in Iowa in the mid-1930s, where he became a proficient horseman. Reagan cheated on his eye exam to get his second lieutenant's commission. His bad eyesight was discovered when World War II broke out, which is why he was confined to a noncombat role in the United States. Churchill wrote, "No one ever came to grief—except honorable grief—through riding horses. No hour of life is lost that is spent in the saddle." Reagan was fond of saying, "There is nothing quite so good for the inside of a man as the outside of a horse"—a phrase most reporters thought Reagan originated but that actually comes from Xenophon's *Art of Horsemanship*.

BOTH MEN HAD their first direct political experience during their college years. In both cases, the cause was dubious and their judgment questionable; in both cases, a rebellious, anti-authoritarian streak that characterized their later political careers was evident. During Reagan's first year at Eureka College in 1928, financial hardships forced Eureka's president, Bert Wilson, to propose severe cutbacks that included faculty layoffs and a contraction of the curriculum. (Among the proposed cutbacks was the home economics department, which, Wilson correctly argued, did not belong at a liberal arts college.) Students and faculty joined together to form a "strike committee" to protest the planned cuts and force Wilson to back down. Wilson rejected an alternative plan the students and faculty committee put forth, and ignored their petition to reconsider the whole matter. Eureka's trustees then approved Wilson's plan.

The "strike committee" escalated, calling for a student boycott of classes and Wilson's resignation. In fact, Wilson had already quietly offered his resignation to Eureka's trustees so that he would not be a lightning rod as the painful reorganization plan went into effect. At an outdoor student rally right after the trustees' vote, Reagan was one of the speakers at the rally, selected, one of his classmates told Garry Wills, because Reagan "was the biggest mouth of the freshman class; he was a cocky s.o.b., a loud talker. Dutch was the guy you wanted to put up there."[4] Reagan recalled the experience vividly: "I discovered that night that an audience has a feel to it and, in the parlance of the theater, the audience and I were together. . . . They came to their feet with a roar. . . . It was heady wine. Hell, with two more lines I could have had them riding through 'every Middlesex village and farm'—without horses yet."[5] (One can see here a clear foreshadowing of Reagan's populist theme of the 1970s about igniting a "prairie fire" across America.) Wilson resigned three weeks later and his planned cuts were scaled back. Edmund Morris called it Reagan's "first lesson in deficit crisis management."[6]

The exact words of Reagan's maiden political speech are unrecorded. Not so for Churchill; his maiden political speech in 1894 was set down word for word—by Churchill himself, naturally. His first public political proclamation was "Ladies of the Empire, I stand for Liberty!" While this sounds like a

straightforward association with the tradition of classical liberalism, in fact the "ladies" Churchill referenced were "ladies
of the night"—prostitutes—and the "Empire" was not the
British colonies but a bawdy music hall in London where
Churchill and other Sandhurst cadets liked to take in the oc-
casional show. When a crusader against vice had succeeded in
shrouding the promenade of the Empire Theatre behind a
cloth barricade, Churchill took up the cause of what he called
"a serious constitutional argument upon the inherent rights of
British subjects; upon the dangers of State interference with
the social habits of law-abiding persons, and upon the many
evil consequences which inevitably follow upon repression
not supported by healthy public opinion." Pure humbug in
this context, but nonetheless the nineteen-year-old Churchill
spent three days writing and revising the speech he would
give at a rally to be sponsored by the Entertainments
Protective League—an ad hoc organization that turned out to
consist of just one rather eccentric older man.[7] When the
Entertainments Protective League effort came to naught,
Churchill took it upon himself to organize a public protest—a
riot, he hoped—at the site of the Empire Theatre. As a mob of
200 to 300 students tore down the flimsy sheet that consti-
tuted the barricade outside the theater, Churchill gave his
speech, which, he says, "was received with rapturous applause. . . . It reminded me of the death of Julius Caeser when
the conspirators rushed forth into the street waving the
bloody daggers with which they had slain the tyrant. I thought
also of the taking of the Bastille. . . . We all sallied out into
[Leicester] Square brandishing fragments of wood and canvas
as trophies or symbols." But London was safe from further
revolution that night: "We had to catch the last train back to
Sandhurst or be guilty of dereliction of duty."[8] Within days a

permanent barricade went up outside the Empire Theatre. Not for nothing does Aristotle write that the young are unsuited to politics.

IF THE FORMAL education of Reagan and Churchill provides little clue to their future political genius, then one must look for insights to their informal self-education in politics during adulthood. Here we find a gold mine. Following his studies at Sandhurst, Churchill considered applying to Oxford or Cambridge, but he was deterred by his fear of the Greek and Latin prerequisites on the entrance exams. The world beyond Sandhurst, Churchill wrote, "opened like Aladdin's Cave"—a phrase perhaps deliberately reminiscent of the emergence from Plato's cave in *The Republic*. In 1896, at age twenty-two, he went off to his first military posting in Bangalore, India, where, he later wrote, "I began to feel myself wanting in even the vaguest knowledge about many large spheres of thought."[9] In other words, Churchill recognized that his formal education had been inadequate for a would-be politician. "So I resolved to read history, philosophy, economics, and things like that. . . . It was a curious education. First because I approached it with an empty, hungry mind, and with fairly strong jaws; and what I got I bit; secondly because I had no one to tell me: 'This is discredited.' 'You should read the answer to that by so and so.' 'There is a much better book on that subject,' and so forth.' " In other words, Churchill had the graduate student's reading list without the stifling guild mentality of the graduate faculty.[10]

In the hot Indian afternoons, when most British subalterns rested or slept in the shade, Churchill read as much as five hours a day, often "three or four books at a time to avoid tedium." To remedy the gaps in his historical knowledge,

Churchill read all eight volumes of Gibbon's *Decline and Fall of the Roman Empire.* After Gibbon, Churchill tackled Macaulay's works (including Macaulay's severe criticism of Churchill's ancestor, the first Duke of Marlborough), William Lecky's *History of European Morals,* and Henry Hallam's *Constitutional History of England.* In philosophy and science, Churchill read Plato's *Republic* and *Symposium,* Aristotle's *Politics,* Schopenhauer, Pascal, John Stuart Mill, Adam Smith's *Wealth of Nations,* Thomas Malthus, Charles Darwin, and Laing's *Modern Science and Modern Thought.* (He had already been introduced to the works of Edmund Burke by an American, ironically enough, the New York grandee Bourke Cochran. Cochran was a major influence on Churchill's public speaking style.) Churchill "blended them all," Kenneth Thompson wrote in an extensive study of Churchill's thought, "into a version of man and politics that became uniquely his own."[11] Churchill would later describe his own writing style as a combination of Macaulay and Gibbon.

One important political book that we know Churchill read either at Bangalore or shortly after, but which he omits to mention anywhere in his memoirs, is Machiavelli's *The Prince,* often called "the most famous book about politics ever written." We know Churchill read Machiavelli because a few years later, in the early years of his career as a member of Parliament and then as a junior cabinet minister, he frequently sent copies of the book to friends along with his endorsement of the book's value. Machiavelli and the adjective made from his name—*Machiavellian*—have a sinister connotation in political life, and Churchill was undoubtedly aware of this.

Churchill supplemented his reading of classic texts with a close study of contemporary British politics. He did this through the most extraordinary means: he had his mother ship him 27 volumes of the *Annual Register*—the British equivalent of the *Congressional Record*—which contains the transcripts of parliamentary debate over several previous decades. Churchill read the parliamentary debates assiduously, and wrote out speeches and talking points he would have used in the debates himself.

Churchill reflected deeply on his reading, and wrote long letters to his mother detailing his unfolding political views, and also his reflections on political oratory. (The course of Churchill's political thought will be considered in Chapter 6.) Churchill did not read novels, but he started writing one, which eventually became his only work of published fiction, *Savrola*. As would be expected from a young writer, it was closely autobiographical and offers additional clues about his self-education. ("All my philosophy is put into the mouth of my hero," Churchill wrote his mother about the novel.)

Reagan's political self-education occurred later in life than Churchill's. As we know, Reagan came to adulthood as an admirer of Franklin Roosevelt and the New Deal—another similarity to Churchill. As of the end of the 1940s, Reagan could still describe himself as a "near hopeless hemophiliac liberal." Reagan's change of mind from the left to the right will be considered more fully in Chapter 6; what is important to understand at this point is that he did it himself. Reagan's detractors have long assumed that someone—his second wife, Nancy, perhaps—talked him out of his liberalism. Reagan himself explained it in 1976: "Eventually what happened to me was, because I did my own speeches and did the research for them, I just woke up to the realization one day that I had been going out and helping to elect the people who had been causing the things I had been criticizing. So it wasn't any case of some mentor coming in and talking me out of it. I did it in my own speeches."[12]

The key period of Reagan's political self-education was in the 1950s. As the host of *GE Theater* on TV, Reagan traveled the nation speaking at General Electric manufacturing plants in more than thirty states. Reagan made all these travels by train because he was afraid to fly (a fear he conquered only when his political ambition made flying necessary).[13] His GE traveling companion, Earl Dunckel, recalled that Reagan spent much of his time on the long train trips reading books and magazines and writing his speeches.

We do not know Reagan's reading list during this period. Unlike Churchill, Reagan offered few recollections of key books. (To the contrary, Reagan took pains to avoid revealing his reading habits. Late in his presidency, his press aide Marlin Fitzwater noticed Reagan was reading several serious current books—as opposed to the Louis L'Amour novels Reagan often admitted to reading. Fitzwater asked Reagan if the press office could put out a media advisory about his current reading—Clinton used to do this routinely—as a way of combating the widespread criticism that Reagan was out of touch and uncurious about the world. Reagan replied, "No, Marlin, I don't think we need to do that."[14]) We know about a couple of titles Reagan read during that time, including Whittaker Chambers's *Witness,* from which he could quote long passages from memory years later. But from his subsequent speeches and articles it is possible to guess that he read a number of now-classic conservative and libertarian books, such as Henry Hazlitt's *Economics in One Lesson,* F. A. Hayek's *The Road to Serfdom,* Milton Friedman's *Capitalism and Freedom,* and especially the little-known nineteenth-century

French liberal Claude-Frédéric Bastiat. We also know Reagan also was an early reader of *National Review* following its founding in 1955, and *The Freeman,* the periodical of the libertarian Foundation for Economic Education.

References to Bastiat sprinkle Reagan's speeches, original radio addresses, and articles. Another direct parallel: Churchill also read and quoted from Bastiat in his defense of free trade starting in 1903. It is doubtful there has ever been another prominent American political figure, let alone a president, who quoted Bastiat. (Reagan also occasionally quoted an obscure Arab economist named Ibn-Khaldun.) But Reagan derived more than aphorisms from his reading. Like Churchill in Bangalore, Reagan didn't have anyone to tell him that these authors were beyond the pale or discredited in some way. Or he ignored the established intellectual authorities who did.

In both cases Reagan's and Churchill's self-study contributed directly to their independent and unconventional views. In Churchill's case, his study and military experience combined to generate, in the words of Isaiah Berlin, "a historical imagination so strong, so comprehensive, as to encase the whole of the present and the whole of the future in a framework of a rich and multicolored past." One of Churchill's favorite axioms was "The longer you look back, the farther you can look forward." It is significant that while Churchill wrote that genius cannot be taught, late in life, when a group of students asked him how they should prepare for a political career, Churchill answered with two words: "Study history." On another occasion he remarked, "A good knowledge of history is a quiver full of arrows in debate." And on still another occasion, he argued, "Knowledge of the past is the only foundation we have from which to peer into and measure the future. Expert knowledge, however indispensable, is no substitute for a generous and comprehending outlook upon the human story with all its sadness and with all its unquench-able hope."[15]

Reagan's imagination had a historical dimension, too, though not as deep or wide-ranging as Churchill's. As Lou Cannon put it, "Reagan spoke to the future with the accents of the past." George Will's equally serviceable formula was "He does not want to return to the past; he wants to return to the past's way of facing the future."

Reagan's capacious imagination is most often attributed to the make-believe world of Hollywood movies. This unjustly slights his reading and self-education. In part this is because Reagan concealed his reading habits. But his long Hollywood experience is certainly part of the source of his imagination. Tony Dolan, one of Reagan's chief speechwriters, pointed out, "Actors get used to alternate endings." It is because Reagan had overcome the unlucky episodes in his life that he retained his optimism and imagination. At every point of Reagan's life where his progress might have ended, he made for himself a new story line. Alternative endings to a drama require positive acts of imagination that must nonetheless be rooted in reality. Reagan transferred this from his personal life to his political outlook. What he saw as a real potentiality for the Cold War, conservative tragedians and conventional political thinkers saw as a flight of fancy. Audacity, to paraphrase an old cliché, consists of knowing the difference between potentiality and flights of fancy when no one else around you can.

Because Reagan acquired a reputation as an anti-intellectual lightweight, his actions and decisions were often attributed to his advisers, or "handlers." As Lou Cannon put it, "The prevailing view in Washington became that what the people most often saw was the work of his staff, his cabinet, his political advisers or his wife." Cannon is not alone in coming to see that this perception was wrong. While Reagan was a good listener and was open to persuasion, he could also be stubborn. He refused to budge on his core ideas, no matter how unanimous the advice to the contrary from his staff and cabinet. "As president," Cannon observed, "he was at once the most malleable and the least moveable of men." Most frustrating to Reagan's staff and political opponents alike was the unfathomable nature of this thought process. "The nature of Reagan's intellect remains a puzzlement," Cannon wrote. "It was clear to me that he was not a dunce . . . but it was difficult to understand how his mind worked. . . . [Reagan had] power of analysis without possessing any visible analytical ability." This is too harsh, but only by a little. While Reagan's writings display conventional analytical ability, as president he tended to employ analysis-by-anecdote in his personal interaction with others. (Is this really so different from Churchill? Churchill once explained his own thought process this way: "I have often tried to set down the strategic truths I have comprehended in the form of simple anecdotes.")

Cannon eventually came to subscribe to the view of Harvard psychologist Howard Gardner, who argues that Reagan had an essentially narrative rather than conventionally deductive imagination (this would apply to Churchill as well). Economist Annelise Anderson, who served Reagan at the Office of Management and Budget, said that Reagan thought in concrete examples rather than abstractions. (This parallels Harold Laski's complaint that "Mr. Churchill has not a speculative mind; with him a theory begets not interest but suspicion.") Despite all these peculiarities, Cannon concluded that the decisive factor was that Reagan had good judgment and "was abundantly endowed with common sense."

Churchill's wartime image of stubborn resolve obscures the ways in which his contemporaries described his thought process in terms very similar to how Reagan's were described. John Colville, a close aide to Churchill during World War II and again in the 1950s, wrote:

> He has always retained unswerving independence of thought. He approached a problem as he himself saw it and of all the men I have ever known he was least liable to be swayed by the views of even his most intimate counselors. Many people made the mistake of thinking that somebody—it might be General Ismay or Professor Lindemann—for whom the Prime Minister had the utmost respect and affection, would be able to "get something through." Unless the Prime Minister was himself impressed by the argument, pressure by others seldom had any effect. If a subject bored him he would pass it, however important, to somebody else for a decision and would scarcely pause to consider the grounds on which that decision had been reached. But once his personal attention was engaged he had to be convinced that his initial reaction was wrong before he could agree to change his line. He was open to persuasion, although it often needed courage to press the point, but he was never persuaded by the fact that those who argued a certain course were people whom he liked and respected. There were indeed a number of occasions when he showed a quite inexplicable facility for reaching the right decision on faulty logic and against all the best advice.[16]

THEIR DIFFERENT CHILDHOODS and self-educations created similar outlooks and bold imaginations, but Reagan and Churchill differed sharply in their religious views, as we will see in the next chapter. Yet both ended up with a similar sense of personal and national destiny.

CHAPTER 5

Faith and Destiny

I have fallen back reposefully into the arms of fate, but with an underlying instinct that all will be well.

—WINSTON CHURCHILL, 1915

When the Lord calls me home, whenever that may be, I will leave with the greatest love for this country of ours and eternal optimism for its future. . . . I know that for America there will always be a bright dawn ahead.

—RONALD REAGAN,
FINAL LETTER TO THE AMERICAN PEOPLE, 1994

No ASPECT of a person's views and character can be more difficult to penetrate than religion. On the subject of religion, a conspicuous difference between Reagan and Churchill seems to emerge, though on closer inspection their differences dissolve and then converge in terms of personal and national destiny, which both men understood in transcendent ways. Both men were almost mystical—a common trait in great figures throughout history.

On the surface, Christian faith appears to play a much

larger role in Reagan's life than in Churchill's. Churchill displayed a nonchalant attitude toward religion throughout much of his life, recording in *My Early Life* that he adopted "Low Church" principles from his antipapist governess, Miss Everett, and allowing that he purposely misbehaved in mandatory chapel in school. He seldom attended church as an adult, and occasionally affected an impious pose, commenting once, "I am ready to meet my maker; whether my maker is ready to meet me is another question." When asked about his religious views, Churchill would defer by quoting Disraeli: "Sensible men are all of the same religion." And what religion would that be? "Sensible men never tell."[1]

As he aged, Churchill gave some indications of acquiring conventional piety. John Colville recorded in his diary, "As regards religion he was an agnostic who, as the years went by, and I think more particularly as a result of the Battle of Britain, slowly began to conceive that there was some overriding power which had a conscious influence on our destinies." Maybe, Churchill speculated to Colville in the 1950s, heaven was a constitutional monarchy, "in which case there was always a possibility that the Almighty might have occasion to 'send for him.' "[2]

Reagan was a regular churchgoer throughout his adult life, except during the White House years, when he seldom attended church because of the disruption his security arrangements inevitably imposed on the congregation or parish. This led to criticism, including from a few ideological allies, that Reagan was insincere or only lightly religious. To be sure, although Reagan quoted the Bible from memory from time to time, he displayed few of the mannerisms of Protestant evangelicalism. "He had no use for organized religion," Lou Cannon wrote, "though he said he often prayed." His wife's fascination with astrology was thought to be taken more seriously as an influence on his presidency. His private correspondence, especially during his presidency, displays a deep personal religious faith. "I believe the Bible is the result of Divine inspiration and is *not* just a history," Reagan wrote to a correspondent in 1967. "I believe in it."[3] After his narrow loss to Gerald Ford in the 1976 nomination fight, Reagan expressed both his faith and his sense of destiny to a correspondent who had sent good wishes: "Whether it is this job or whether it is early training from long ago just now coming clear, I find myself believing very deeply that God has a plan for each of us. Some with little faith and even less testing seem to miss it in their mission, or perhaps we fail to see the imprint on the lives of others. But bearing what we cannot change, going on with what God has given us, confident there is a destiny, somehow seems to bring a reward we wouldn't exchange for any other. *It takes a lot of fire and heat to make a piece of steel* [emphasis added]."[4]

Reagan's public reserve about his personal faith is thought to be another aspect of his remoteness or his slightly shy personality, but it is also true that he saw his restraint as a corrective to what he considered Jimmy Carter's public abuse of religious faith during Carter's presidency. The contrast between the two men could hardly be more instructive: Carter invoked his religious faith to bolster his own claims to personal virtue; Reagan decided to downplay his personal religious faith, and invoked religious faith to bolster the claims of *America's* virtue instead of his own.

Reagan seldom made a speech that did not include some divine reference, a trait that was not lost on the Soviets. Soviet spokesman Anatoly Krasikov noted in 1986, "Whenever Mr. Reagan delivers a speech, he always mentions his religious feelings."[5] Reagan's religious faith was the basis of his strongest hatred for Communism: the express atheism of Communism offended him more than garden-variety tyranny. In his most famous speech attacking the Soviet Union, the "evil empire" speech of March 1983, Reagan said, "Yes, let us pray for the salvation of all of those who live in that totalitarian darkness—pray they will discover the joy of knowing God. But until they do, let us be aware that while they preach the supremacy of the state, declare its omnipotence over individual man, and predict its eventual domination of all peoples on the Earth, they are the focus of evil in the modern world."

Churchill was also fervently anti-Communist, having railed against "Bolshevism" (as he called it for years) from the moment of its inception in Russia in 1917. Churchill's visceral hatred of Communism practically exhausted his extensive vocabulary. Like Reagan, he referred to the Soviet Union as a regime of unvarnished "evil." Most of Churchill's public criticism of Communism and Fascism in the 1920s and 1930s harked back to the classical understanding of tyranny or despotism as a violent and corrupt form of rule. But like Reagan he also objected to Communism's explicit denial of the right of conscience. "We defend freedom of conscience and religious equality," Churchill said of the infant Soviet regime in 1920. "They seek to exterminate every form of religion that has given comfort and inspiration to the soul of man."[6]

YET IF REAGAN was more outwardly devout, Churchill offered a more extensive account of his contemplation of religion than Reagan did. Churchill held a classical view of the dynamic tension between faith and reason and an appreciation for G. K. Chesterton–style paradox. In *My Early Life* he confesses to adopting "a predominantly secular view," and having for a time "passed through a violent and aggressive anti-religious phase."[7] But he quickly came to reject the conventional modern view that science and reason had superseded religious teaching and religious belief. "The idea that nothing is true except when we comprehend is silly," he wrote, "and that ideas which our minds cannot reconcile are mutually destructive, sillier still."[8] He wrote an essay about the leadership of Moses in which he dismisses modern biblical criticism for controverting pious respect for the Bible and diluting belief in the plain narrative of Judaeo-Christian antiquity.[9] Then in *Closing the Ring*, the fifth volume of *The Second World War*, Churchill returns to the theme of reason and faith with a seemingly incidental observation: "No two cities have counted for more with mankind than Athens and Jerusalem. Their messages in religion, philosophy, and art have been the main guiding lights of modern faith and culture." This is an implicit rejection of modernity, since it is *ancient* Athens and *ancient* Jerusalem that Churchill has in mind here.[10] The uneasy and hard-bought harmony of these two traditions was shattered by the Enlightenment, and the medieval synthesis of faith and reason is championed today chiefly among Roman Catholics, which puts Churchill in unexpected company.

The most revealing formulation of Churchill's views on the crossroads of religion and politics comes in *The Gathering Storm*, the first volume of *The Second World War*, in his famous discussion of the 1938 Munich agreement that handed over Czechoslovakia to Hitler: "The Sermon on the Mount is the last word in Christian ethics. Everyone respects the Quakers. Still, *it is not on these terms that Ministers assume their responsibilities of guiding states* [emphasis added]." Churchill goes on to offer an unacknowledged paraphrase of a Machiavellian axiom: "There is no merit in putting off a war for a year if, when it comes, it is a far worse war or one much harder to win." (Machiavelli wrote in *The Prince:* "A disorder should never be allowed to continue so as to avoid a war, because that is not to avoid it but to defer it to your disadvantage.")

Churchill continues, "It is baffling to reflect that what men call honor does not correspond always to Christian ethics." Had France and England followed the path of honor, which pointed to the path of duty, Churchill suggested, Hitler might have been stopped once and for all in 1938. The policy of appeasement that led to the catastrophe of Munich drew some of its support from Christian pacifism, just as much of the opposition to Reagan's military buildup in the 1980s did. Churchill's recognition that *honor* is not a Christian virtue is a discussion straight from the Middle Ages, at a time when a distinction between the City of God and the City of Man was more central to political thought—paradoxically a time when religious and civil authority tended to be inextricably mixed (think "Holy Roman Empire").

An ironic result of the modern formal separation of church and state that guaranteed freedom of conscience for individuals is that it had the collateral effect of widening the dynamic tension between Christian virtues (especially the virtues of love and humility) and classical virtues (especially magnanimity and honor). Nations have a life beyond individuals, and are not subject to Christian salvation and redemption. The self-preservation of a nation, especially a decent nation that observes freedom of religion, has a different rank on the hierarchy of ethics than the self-preservation of an individual. Christian teaching cannot resolve this difficulty. Churchill recognized that this was a "tormenting dilemma" for statesmen, because in most cases "religion and virtue alike lend their sanctions to meekness and humility, *not only between men but between nations* [emphasis added]."

But under extreme circumstances—such as when confronted by Hitler or the Soviet Union—Christian and classical ethics may demand divergent paths. Churchill cannot resolve this problem either: "No case of this kind can be judged apart from its circumstances." One can speculate, however, that had Churchill been prime minister in 1938, and taken Britain and France into a "preemptive" war against Germany at that time, he might well be remembered poorly today as someone who overreacted and started an unnecessary war, just as President George W. Bush is charged with doing in the case of Iraq.

Although Reagan never articulated his reflections on any potential conflict between biblical morality and the requirements of national honor, he clearly thought along the same lines as Churchill. His administration and his supporters went to great lengths in the early 1980s to counter the pacifism of the Catholic bishops and the antinuclear movement that opposed Reagan's ultimately successful strategy of building up arms to pressure the Soviet Union to stop its own ominous buildup.

Whatever the character of their most private spiritual thoughts, both men shared a conception of transcendent Providence that led to an overpowering sense of personal destiny. In both cases it is possible to discern that their shared sense of destiny was connected in substantive ways to their character and their philosophical outlook—their sense of personal destiny merged inevitably into their belief in national destiny.

Churchill was certain he was destined for high office and greatness from an early age, though this confidence did desert him on a few occasions during his "wilderness years" in the 1930s. One of the most remarkable foreshadowings of Churchill's future came in a throwaway passage in the original edition of his 1900 book, *The River War.* This book was Churchill's account of Britain's reconquest of the Sudan in 1898, in which Churchill participated in what is sometimes said to have been the last cavalry charge ever made by the British army.[11] The Sudan campaign pitted the vastly superior forces and firepower of the British army against an Islamic army that might, with due allowance, be considered the al Qaeda of its day. They were known as the "Dervishes" for their manner of waving their scimitars above their heads while loudly screaming. At a late point in the battle, by which time there was no doubt of the outcome, a last contingent of "Dervishes" made a futile charge into the British lines, and were slaughtered to the last man. Churchill takes care to praise their futile courage: "The valour of their deed has been discounted by those who have told their tale. 'Mad fanaticism' is the deprecating comment of their conquerers. I hold this to be a cruel injustice. Nor can he be a very brave man who will not credit them with a nobler motive, and believe that they died to clear their honour from the stain of defeat. Why should we regard as madness in the savage what would be sublime in civilized men?" But then Churchill goes on to add this remarkable premonition: *"For I hope that if evil days should come upon our own country, and the last army which a collapsing Empire could interpose between London and the invader were dissolving in rout and ruin, that there would be some—even in these modern days—who would not care to accustom themselves to a new order of things and tamely survive the disaster* [emphasis added]."

Who does this sound like, if not the defiant Churchill of 1940? In the summer of 1940, with a German invasion expected to begin at any moment, Churchill prepared a speech to be broadcast as the invasion began. His working title for the speech was "You Can Take One with You." Women can grab a kitchen knife and stab a German soldier, he suggested.

One of Churchill's most famous passages is the last paragraph of *The Gathering Storm*, where he wrote of the night he became prime minister, May 10, 1940, hours after the German invasion of France had begun: "I felt as if I were walking with destiny, and that all of my past life had been but a preparation for this hour and this trial." Of course, these words were written after the war, with the benefit of hindsight. But there are many contemporaneous accounts of Churchill's belief in his own destiny. A few days after he became prime minister, Churchill said to his doctor, Lord Moran, "This cannot be an accident, it must be design. I was kept for this job."

If Churchill was slightly irreligious or agnostic, his reflections on destiny turned his thoughts to a "higher power" that, like Aristotle, he was tempted to ascribe to a generic God. In *My Early Life* he reflected on the month he spent—before escaping—from a Boer prisoner-of-war camp in 1899: "I realized with awful force that no exercise of my feeble wit and strength could save me from my enemies, and that without the assistance of that High Power which interferes in the eternal sequence of causes and effects more often than we are always prone to admit, I could never succeed."[12]

Churchill returned to this theme numerous times throughout his life. After an episode in World War I where an unexpected request for a meeting from a higher officer saved Churchill from being killed by an artillery shell that struck his headquarters moments after he departed, he reflected again on what it meant: "Chance, Fortune, Luck, Destiny, Fate, Providence seem to me only different ways of expressing the same thing, to wit, that a man's own contribution to his life story is continually dominated by an external superior power."[13]

Reagan offered fewer personal reflections about his personal destiny, though he said publicly on several occasions that he thought the presidency sought the man. This might be depreciated as false modesty from someone whose campaign strategy emphasized that he was not a career politician. He did say to both Mike Deaver and Lyn Nofziger in 1968, however, that he was relieved that he didn't get the Republican nomination that year, because he wasn't ready to be president yet. (Reagan came closer to derailing Richard Nixon's nomination than is commonly recalled.) But after he survived the assassin's bullet in 1981, few questioned Reagan's sincerity when he said that he thought God had spared his life for a purpose — the purpose of ending the Cold War.

A fragment from Reagan's biography that bears on his education, religious faith, and sense of destiny can be found in his encounter, at age eleven, with a popular moral story of the time, Harold Bell Wright's *That Printer of Udell's*. The story is eerily similar to Reagan's own, opening with a scene of a boy standing over the expiring body of his alcoholic father in a scene similar to what Reagan experienced with his own father at roughly the same time he read Wright's book. The boy in the story grows up, moves to the big city, overcomes hardship and poverty to become a tradesman (the printer of the title), and then becomes politically active, urging his fellow citizens in a speech to make provisions for the poor among them. (Consistent with the Reagan of his later political career, the protagonist of *That Printer of Udell's* urges private charity, rather than public assistance, for the city's poor and downtrodden, in part out of concern for the dignity of the recipient.) He finds religion and a loyal wife along the way, and the story ends with the city voting to send him to Washington, D.C.

Coincidence? Perhaps, but Reagan said to his mother after finishing the book, "I want to be like that man." Reagan still talked about *That Printer of Udell's* fifty years later, telling biographer Edmund Morris that reading Wright's book made him "a practical Christian." He also said the book prompted his decision to be baptized in his mother's church, the Disciples of Christ. During his presidency Reagan wrote to Wright's daughter-in-law, telling her, "I had found a role model in that traveling printer Harold Bell Wright had brought to life. He set me on a course I've tried to follow even unto this day. I shall always be grateful."[14]

Reagan's belief in the destiny of the United States was vividly expressed in religious language. His most famous religious imagery was his often-used fragment from the famous John Winthrop sermon from 1630 about America as "a city on a hill." He also liked to quote from Pope Pius XII: "Into the hands of America God has placed the destinies of an afflicted mankind." This was not a new theme that began with his political career. In a commencement address at William Woods College in 1952 (given coincidentally in Fulton, Missouri, near the site of Churchill's Iron Curtain speech), Reagan expressed his providential understanding of America: "I in my own mind have thought of America as a place in the divine scheme of things that was set aside as a promised land. . . . I believe that God in shedding his grace on this country has always in this divine scheme of things kept an eye on our land and guided it as a promised land."

Churchill shared Reagan's views about the destiny of the United States to be the beacon of freedom for the entire world. Churchill's rhetoric about the "special relationship" or the destiny of the "English-speaking peoples" is sometimes attributed to the fact that Churchill was half-American himself, or dismissed as the necessity of flattery on the part of a declining power that needed the help of the United States to survive. Certainly there were tensions between the lingering vestiges of the British empire and the anti-imperial views of U.S. foreign policy that occasionally troubled relations between Churchill and Roosevelt. A closer look will show, however, that Churchill's view was sincerely held, and based on a deep understanding of America and America's principles. It is at this point that the closest similarity between Churchill's and Reagan's conservatism emerges.

CHAPTER 6

The Path to Conservatism:
The Political Parallels

He who is not a liberal at 20 has no heart; he who is not a conservative at 40 has no brains.

—ATTRIBUTED TO CHURCHILL

PRESS QUESTION: *Mr. President, in talking about the continuing recession tonight, you have blamed mistakes of the past, and you've blamed the Congress. Does any of the blame belong to you?*
PRESIDENT REAGAN: *Yes, because for many years I was a Democrat. [Laughter.]*

—WHITE HOUSE PRESS CONFERENCE,
SEPTEMBER 28, 1982

WINSTON CHURCHILL stunned the political world when, as a young member of Parliament in 1904, he "crossed the aisle" to switch from his father's Conservative Party to the Liberal Party. It was the first of two party switches Churchill made; as he put it, he "ratted and re-ratted." He rejoined the Conservative Party twenty years later, where, never trusted by the party establishment, he drew what

91

little support he had from the far-right wing of the party. He was always the outsider, the rebel, a thorn in the side of the party leadership. "The Conservatives have never liked nor trusted me," Churchill wrote in the 1920s. He remained a figure of suspicion within his own party even after he became prime minister in 1940. It is forgotten today that Churchill was widely expected to fail as prime minister when he took the job in 1940. According to his biographer, King George VI was "bitterly opposed" to Churchill's becoming prime minister. One of the cabinet secretaries, John Colville, wrote that there had been an air of "malaise" around the previous prime minister, Neville Chamberlain. But Churchill would be worse, Colville thought: "In May 1940 the mere thought of Churchill as Prime Minister sent a cold chill down the spines of the staff working at 10 Downing Street. . . . Seldom can a Prime Minister have taken office with the Establishment . . . so dubious of the choice and so prepared to find its doubts justified."[1] "This is not the last war administration by a long way," a leading member of Churchill's own party remarked. Another Tory MP, Peter Eckersley, wrote, "Winston won't last five months! Opposition from Tories is already beginning." MP David Kier wrote in his diary a month after Churchill took office, "The more I think of the position, the more uncertain the future of Winston's present Government is." Among other things, Churchill, at age sixty-five, was thought to be too old for the rigors of wartime office.

Fifty years after Churchill's first party switch, across the Atlantic and on the far side of the North American continent, Democrats in Los Angeles looking for a congressional candidate in the 1950s considered asking Ronald Reagan to make a run. The idea was rejected: Reagan was "too liberal." When he switched parties a decade later and ran successfully for governor of California, Reagan drew his strength from the right wing of the Republican Party, and was regarded even within his own party as a dangerous fringe figure. Even after two successful terms as governor of the largest state in the union, the GOP establishment regarded a Reagan candidacy for president in 1976 as a menace to the party. The Ripon Society huffed that "the nomination of Ronald Reagan would McGovernize the Republican Party. . . . Reagan is today unsuited for major responsibility in any area bearing on diplomacy or the conduct of foreign policy." Vice President Nelson Rockefeller dismissed Reagan as "a minority of a minority," and charged that Reagan "has been taking some extreme positions." Republican senator Jacob Javits devoted an entire speech to an attack on Reagan. Reagan's positions, he said, were "so extreme that they would alter our country's very economic and social structure and our place in the world to such a degree as to make our country's policy at home and abroad, as we know it, a thing of the past." Republican senator Charles Percy issued a statement calling Reagan's candidacy "foolhardy," and predicting Reagan's nomination would lead to "crushing defeat" for the GOP: "It could signal the beginning of the end of our party as an effective force in American political life."

In the nomination contest of 1980 the Republic establishment would have preferred Gerald Ford, Howard Baker, or George Bush to Reagan if they had had it in their power to determine the nomination themselves. Reagan was not the man to cure the nation's "malaise" that his predecessor detected. Among other things, Reagan, at age sixty-nine, was thought too old for the rigors of the presidency. "Reagan's election,"

John P. Roche, a former head of the liberal Americans for
Democratic Action, wrote in 1984, "was thus an 8-plus earth-
quake on the political Richter scale, and it sent a number
of eminent statesmen—Republican and Democratic—into
shock." Skeptics were legion. *Los Angeles Times* White House
reporter Jack Nelson recalled that "few political observers
gave Reagan much chance of exerting strong leadership" at
the time of his election.[2] Senator Gary Hart said, "I give the
Reagan Administration about 18 to 24 months to prove that it
doesn't have any answers either." Sociologist Alan Wolfe predicted in *The Nation* that "Ronald Reagan will slide America
deeper into its decline."[3] Political scientist Curtis Gans wrote
that "there is nothing in the Republican outlook on either the
American economy or foreign affairs that suggests the party
can successfully govern for any long period of time."[4]

Churchill and Reagan defied their doubters. Even critics
of their political views generally agree that they succeeded at
many (not all) of their larger aims. Churchill's genius and skill
were always widely acknowledged. Reagan's case remains
more ambiguous; the lightness of his bearing still gives the
impression of legerdemain; many in the media and in acade-
mia still believe his success was some combination of luck and
strong staff support. Clark Clifford's famous early dismissal of
Reagan as an "amiable dunce" has had a long half-life. Yet
Cold War historian Derek Leebaert sums up Reagan this way:
"It is beyond the laws of probability to believe that this was all
coincidence or a matter of being lucky. . . . The lack of surface
arrogance should not conceal his force of will, nor his modesty in details obscure a confidence in his contribution to the
heart of things such as only great men or fools possess. The
hypothesis of foolishness becomes weaker by the day."[5]

In the end the success of a statesman depends on more

than political skill. Insight and conviction must inform political skill. And again the parallels between Reagan's and Churchill's political convictions and insights are more substantial the more extensively they are seen side by side. A closer look reveals that these great champions of conservatism worked out their own highly idiosyncratic conservative philosophies that many of their admirers today still do not recognize or understand.

A sensible comparison begins with the apparent coincidences and ascends into the interstices of their thought on specific issues. The obvious starting point is with the fact that both men were party switchers. As president, Reagan frequently cited the words and example of Churchill whenever he welcomed a party-switching Democrat into the GOP. When Democratic congressman Eugene Atkinson switched parties to become a Republican in 1981, Reagan welcomed him with the comment "In both cases we followed the courage of action characterized so eloquently by Winston Churchill: 'Some men change principle for party and some men charge party for principle.' "

In both cases it is not clear whether either man really changed his views as substantially as we typically think. Both men were fundamentally conservative, as the term is understood today, from the beginning.[6] Even after their party switches, both Churchill and Reagan maintained an ambivalent relationship with their liberal mentors and heroes— David Lloyd George in Churchill's case; Franklin Roosevelt in Reagan's. They alternated between sharp criticism and gestures of fondness for their former heroes. Churchill almost brought Lloyd George back into the cabinet in 1941, and Reagan loved to quote from memory many of FDR's statements criticizing bureaucracy and the welfare state, much to the chagrin of liberals.[7] In his standard campaign stump speech in 1984, Reagan would say, "I began my political life as a Democrat, casting my first vote in 1932 for Franklin Delano Roosevelt." But Reagan would go on to say that it was not he who had changed his mind. Speaking specifically to Democrats in the audience, he would add, "I was a Democrat most of my adult life. I didn't leave my party, and we're not suggesting you leave yours. I am telling you that what I felt was that the leadership of the Democratic Party had left me and millions of patriotic Democrats in this country who believed in freedom."

Reagan's longtime adviser Martin Anderson makes the curious observation that in all his years of working with and studying Reagan, he does not know of a single example of a specific liberal or New Deal policy that Reagan supported or praised. On close inspection Reagan's fondness for FDR can be seen as not merely an appreciation of FDR's personal attributes and political greatness, but also an affinity for the New Deal's *conservative* purposes and effects—a point that ideological conservatives have always been loath to admit, but which has always been the chief complaint against the New Deal on the far Left. In a nutshell, for all of its drive to expand the size of government, the dominant social purpose of the New Deal was the preservation of the middle class. There was a problem, however: the inherent weakness of post–New Deal liberalism was its lack of a limiting principle. There was no social problem for which a centralized government remedy could not be devised.[8] Reagan understood this problem before it became more widely apparent. He made a clear distinction in his own mind between the *social insurance* mentality of New Deal liberalism and the *social engineering* mentality of the

Great Society liberalism that emerged in the 1960s.[9] "The press is trying to paint me as now trying to undo the New Deal," Reagan complained in a diary entry in 1982. "I remind them that I voted for FDR four times. I'm trying to undo the 'Great Society.' It was LBJ's war on poverty that led us to our present mess." This is somewhat disingenuous, of course; Reagan was loudly complaining about big government liberalism long before Johnson's Great Society began. Despite all the complaints about Reagan's social service budget cuts, however, he never enacted a single cut to a New Deal–era social insurance program. It is for reasons such as these that presidential scholar Richard Neustadt could write that Reagan was "a New Deal Republican."

Still, if it is true that it was not Reagan but the character of American liberalism that changed, it still presents a mystery. Reagan's reidentification from a New Deal liberal to a Goldwater conservative in the 1950s is yet another sign that he was ahead of his time. What happened to Reagan ideologically in the 1950s happened to numerous liberal intellectuals in the 1960s and 1970s. Irving Kristol wrote that Reagan was the first "neoconservative"—that is, "a liberal mugged by reality." It is not correct to call Reagan a neoconservative, not merely because of the protean character of neoconservatism, but also because Reagan doesn't fit the intellectual and temperamental prerequisites. Still, Kristol is on to something. At the time Reagan did this, it required some courage. Reagan abandoned his Democratic Party liberalism and joined the Right at a time when the Right was still in the political wilderness and regarded by the respectable elites as beyond the fringe, if not nutty. Even when thoughtful liberals did begin to have misgivings in the 1960s, a few of the rising neoconservatives recog-

nized Reagan as a kindred spirit or as a leader who might stem
the tide. The best example of this phenomenon is James Q.
Wilson, who avowed in his famous 1967 *Commentary* article "A
Guide to Reagan Country" that not only did he not sympa-
thize with Reagan, but that "even if I thought like that, which I
don't, I would never write it down anywhere my colleagues at
Harvard might read it." Wilson is today the Ronald Reagan
Professor of Public Policy at Pepperdine University.

Reagan typically gives scant clues to his change of mind.
In *Where's the Rest of Me?,* he wrote that "the first crack" in his
"staunch liberalism" occurred during his military service in
World War II, when he observed firsthand the perverse incentive structure of the civil service bureaucracy. This did not
stop him, though, from enrolling as a member of the liberal
Americans for Democratic Action after the war, applauding
Hubert Humphrey's civil rights stance at the 1948 Democratic
convention, and campaigning with Harry Truman in 1948 and
with Helen Gahagan Douglas against Richard Nixon in 1950.

It was about this time that he found himself in the 91 percent marginal income tax bracket—a phenomenon that has
turned more than a few liberals into libertarians—and saw the
nature of Communism up close in the efforts of the Communist Party to gain control of several Hollywood labor
unions. Far from being a paranoid misadventure to the
McCarthyite antipodes, this was a serious episode that awakened the political animal in Reagan. Sterling Hayden, one
of the "Hollywood Ten" and an admitted member of the
Communist Party, later said that Communism was stopped in
Hollywood by "a one-man battalion of opposition named
Ronald Reagan." During his GE touring days in the 1950s,
Reagan says he began to experience "the vindictiveness of the
liberal temper." It was about this time that the AFL-CIO

branded Reagan "a strident voice of the right wing lunatic fringe." "Sadly," Reagan wrote, "I have come to realize that a great many so-called liberals aren't liberal—they will defend to the death your right to agree with them."

While Reagan was equivocal about the Democratic Party, he was clear that conservatism today has inherited the best of the liberal tradition, which is why he felt none of the sectarian's hesitation about quoting Thomas Paine or admiring Franklin Roosevelt. "The classic liberal," he wrote in *Where's the Rest of Me?*, "used to be the man who believed the individual was, and should be forever, the master of his destiny. That is now the conservative position. The liberal used to believe in freedom under law. He now takes the ancient feudal position that power is everything. He believes in a stronger and stronger central government, in the philosophy that control is better than freedom. The conservative now quotes Thomas Paine, a long-time refuge of the liberals: 'Government is a necessary evil; let us have as little of it as possible.' "

Reagan's use of Thomas Paine gives one indication that his conservatism was unorthodox. Paine was the antithesis of the proto-conservative Edmund Burke. A number of conservative intellectuals took note of Reagan's use of Paine. George Will complained, "[Reagan] is painfully fond of the least conservative sentiment conceivable, a statement from an anticonservative, Thomas Paine: 'We have it on our power to begin the world over again.' Any time, any place, that is nonsense." Nonsense perhaps, but it was vintage Reagan.

Reagan once said, "I believe the heart and soul of conservatism is libertarianism," but his libertarianism was confined chiefly to economic matters, to which his criticisms of pornography and social permissiveness attest. And he was certainly not a "paleoconservative"; despite his wide reading, Reagan's conservatism did not emerge from the pages of Russell Kirk's *The Conservative Mind.* A copy of Whittaker Chambers's letters to William F. Buckley Jr. *(Odyssey of a Friend)* is on the shelf at Reagan's ranch house. One can imagine that Reagan instinctively understood Chambers's comment to Buckley about Kirk: "Would you charge the beach at Tarawa for *that* conservative position? And neither would I!"

If Reagan defied the usual categories and patterns of conservative thought, one must consider the hypothesis that Reagan represents a woefully unrecognized or unrespected category: Reagan was an *American* conservative. This kind of conservatism is not so much a fusion of the best of the various sects as it is a dialectic, embracing the contradiction of belief in optimism and progress along with the suspicion of human nature that requires limited government. Above all it resists schematic description.

Georges Clemenceau reportedly said that Americans have no capacity for abstract thought, and make bad coffee. Perhaps there is a connection: the quality of American coffee (along with American beer) has improved markedly over the last generation, just as the quality of conservative thought has similarly improved. But most conservative thought still emphasizes its derivation from European sources and outlook, whether it is Hayekian libertarianism or Burkean traditionalism. The original contributions and outlook of the Founders, or of Lincoln, are still treated as poor stepchildren, in part because in practice American conservatism tends to eschew the philosophical abstractions that resolve or envelop contradictions.

The authors of *The Federalist* drew attention to this problem with the famous formulation in Number 51: "But what is government itself but the greatest of all reflections on human nature? If men were angels, no government would be necessary. If angels were to govern men, neither external nor internal controls on government would be necessary." Lincoln seemingly contradicts this with his appeal to "the better angels of our nature," but was he not in harmony with that other *Federalist* passage from Number 55: "As there is a degree of depravity in mankind which requires a certain degree of circumspection and distrust, so there are other qualities in human nature which justify a certain portion of esteem and confidence. Republican government presupposes the existence of these qualities in a higher degree than any other form." Reagan, like Lincoln, was perfectly comfortable with this tension. It is also perhaps the key to understanding why Reagan discerned preternaturally early that the departures from the principles of the American founding implied by the premises of New Deal liberalism would ultimately ruin liberalism.

In other words, Reagan's change of mind can be attributed in part to a historical imagination similar to Churchill's that enabled him to see ahead. (Remember Churchill's axiom from the last chapter: "The farther you look back, the farther you can look ahead.") Ultimately this same dynamic can be observed in Churchill's party-switching and change of views. Churchill offered extended reflections on how and why political figures change their mind in a typically elegant essay entitled "Consistency in Politics," one of the essays collected in *Thoughts and Adventures:* "A change of Party is usually considered a much more serious breach of consistency than a change of view. In fact as long as a man works with a Party he will rarely find himself accused of inconsistency, no matter how widely his opinions at one time on any subject can be shown to have altered. . . . To remain constant when a Party

changes is to excite invidious challenge. Moreover, a separation from Party affects all manner of personal relations and
sunders old comradeship." Clearly Churchill is offering an in-
direct reflection and justification for his own party-switching,
though he does not mention his own case, dwelling instead on
the examples of Edmund Burke, William Gladstone, and
Joseph Chamberlain.

It is a pity Churchill did not discuss his own case directly, for it offers a more compelling rationale for his
changes of mind and party than the dated examples he uses.
His critics chalked up his party-switching to pure ambition
and opportunism, and he was often attacked for having taken
"every position on every issue." But there is a deeper background many observers miss. Throughout Churchill's writing
between the world wars runs a consistent theme that the
scale and circumstances of modern life are becoming too
large for human virtue to control. This is the explicit worry of
a companion essay in *Thoughts and Adventures* called "Mass
Effects in Modern Life." The entire arc of Churchill's career—including his two party switches—can be seen as his
struggle to answer the question of whether "human progress
is the result of the resolves and the deeds of individuals, or
are the resolves and deeds of individuals only the outcome of
time and circumstance."

In the period between the wars Churchill was doubtful
about the answer to this. "I have no hesitation," he wrote in
"Mass Effects in Modern Life," "in ranging myself with those
who view the past history of the world mainly as the tale of
exceptional human beings, whose thoughts, actions, qualities,
virtues, triumphs, weaknesses and crimes have dominated
the fortunes of the race. But we must now ask ourselves
whether powerful changes are not coming to pass, are not al-

ready in progress or indeed far advanced. Is not mankind already escaping from the control of individuals?"[10] At one point in the 1930s, when totalitarianism was on the march in Europe and the Western democracies lacked the will to do anything meaningful to stop it, Churchill even expressed doubts about whether parliamentary democracy was still adequate to modern conditions.[11] Not until Churchill's "finest hour" in World War II is his own question given a definitive answer.

Again we should pause to observe a parallel in Reagan's own thought. While he did not develop his thoughts on the problem of scale in the modern world to the same extent as Churchill, he did worry about the ways in which modern society caused individuals to lose their individuality and become an undifferentiated "mass." Like Churchill he resisted the political implications of the historicist view that humans no longer control their destiny by reason or through their own chosen purposes. This, Reagan saw, is a philosophical cornerstone for the idea of ever-expanding administrative government. "I for one find it disturbing," Reagan said in his famous 1964 speech on behalf of Barry Goldwater, "when a representative refers to the free men and women of this country as 'the masses.' " He returned to this theme repeatedly over the years, remarking, for example, in a 1978 radio address about the variety of citizens he met in his travels, "Some of our social planners refer to them as 'the masses' which only proves that they don't know them. . . . They are not 'the masses,' or as the elitists would have it—'the common man.' They are very uncommon."[12]

With this context in mind, Churchill's changes of mind, as well as party, become more coherent. Thus his understanding of political consistency:

A statesman in contact with the moving current of
events and anxious to keep the ship of state on an
even keel and steer a steady course may lean all his
weight now on one side and now on the other. His
arguments in each case when contrasted can be
shown to be not only very different in character, but
contradictory in spirit and opposite in direction: yet
his object will throughout have remained the same.
His resolves, his wishes, his outlook may have been
unchanged; his methods may be verbally irreconcil-
able. We cannot call this inconsistency. In fact it
may be claimed to be the truest consistency. The
only way a man can remain consistent amid changing circumstances is to change with them while pre-
serving the same dominating purpose.[13]

Like Reagan's, Churchill's career is typically seen as having two phases: an early liberal or even "radical" phase chiefly
concerned with domestic policy, and a later conservative
phase after he changed his chief focus of interest from domestic to foreign policy. His political program as a young Liberal
Party cabinet minister included broadening voting rights,
expanding universal education, mandating an eight-hour
workday, establishing old-age pensions and unemployment
insurance, and endorsing the progressive income tax. Surprisingly, he also endorsed isolationism from European affairs
and frequently opposed military spending. Though these
views came to the fore after his first party switch from the
Conservatives to the Liberals in 1904, he had signaled many
years before that his true political sympathies were with the
Liberals. "I am a Liberal in all but name," Churchill wrote
to his mother in 1897. But for the Liberal Party's views on

home rule for Ireland, Churchill concluded, "I would enter Parliament as a Liberal."

Churchill originally changed parties in 1904 over the specific issue of free trade. The Conservative Party was proposing to abandon its long support of free trade in favor of new tariffs to protect domestic British industry and strengthen the Empire. Churchill's arguments were vivid restatements of the classical free-market case in favor of free trade right out of the pages of Adam Smith or David Ricardo: free trade promoted competition and efficiency, and therefore benefited the consumer and increased total prosperity. "Protection is the art of doing business at a loss," he said in one early free-trade speech. He argued that free trade "enshrines certain central truths, economic truths, and, I think, moral truths." Politically, Churchill argued, embracing protectionism would make the Conservative Party resemble the Republican Party in the United States — "rich, materialist, and secular."

But when Churchill returned to the Conservative Party in 1924, he moderated his opposition to protection (it helped that the Conservative Party had backed away from its previous more sweeping protectionism), and defended some trade barriers as a means of protecting British industry. The changed circumstances of the aftermath of World War I, which saw the British economy struggle in the 1920s and ultimately culminated in the Great Depression in the 1930s, shook Churchill's confidence in his economic views. (A major factor in this change of view was the unfortunate results of returning Britain to the gold standard in 1926, a decision taken when Churchill was serving as chancellor of the exchequer. Churchill later said this was the biggest mistake of his entire career. It was not a mistake Reagan emulated. Although several influential advisers urged Reagan to return to the gold standard—he had expressed support for the idea before he became president—and he appointed a commission to investigate the idea after his election, he let the idea quietly drop.) "The compass has been damaged; the charts are out of date," Churchill said of orthodox economic doctrine in 1930.

Yet even if Churchill's specific views on free trade wavered, a case for his overall consistency could still be made out. The reason for Churchill's new doubts about his economic ideas came from the fact that the distress of British industry after World War I and the deflation that occurred from returning to the gold standard at an incorrect valuation put heavy pressure on Britain's working and middle classes. Churchill's dominant objective in domestic policy was always to alleviate the difficult conditions of the working class and enlarge the middle class. He may have been mistaken that free trade was a cause of England's economic difficulties, but it is clear that the "same dominating purpose" he outlined in "Consistency in Politics" was at the root of his changing view, and not a special-interest calculation.

A broad look at Churchill's domestic-policy philosophy shows it had a fundamentally conservative purpose. (Alternatively he could be called a patrician, and his policies paternalistic—criticisms that were also applied to FDR.) Churchill perceived early the revolutionary fervor that would culminate in the Bolshevik Revolution in Russia in 1917, and feared the possibility it might also come to Britain. The socialist enthusiasm that would soon find organized voice in the Labour Party was beginning to rumble. Churchill warned in a 1908 by-election campaign, "An extreme Socialist policy would plunge the country into a violent struggle." He saw liberal social policy—a moderate welfare state—as a bulwark against socialism and revolution: "Reform is always made to step in to block the path of revolution." In a famous speech in 1908, Churchill offered a concise distinction between his ideal of liberalism and socialism:

> Socialism wants to pull down wealth; Liberalism seeks to raise up poverty. Socialism would destroy private interests—Liberalism would preserve them in the only way they could justly be preserved, by reconciling them with public right. Socialism seeks to kill enterprise. Liberalism seeks to rescue enterprise from the trammels of privilege and preference. Socialism assails the maximum pre-eminence of individuals—Liberalism seeks to build up the minimum standard of the masses. Socialism attacks capital; Liberalism attacks monopoly.[14]

It must be pointed out that the "Liberalism" Churchill invokes refers not merely to the party that bore the name (which is why it is "Liberalism" with a capital "L"), but to the inheritance of the classical liberalism of the eighteenth century, which was undergoing profound transformation at that time. It was not the same liberalism as today's liberalism. Churchill's liberalism was similar to what was being self-consciously called "progressivism" in the United States at the same time—a more moderate, ameliorative liberalism aimed at expanding individual opportunity and middle-class security. The ambiguity and incoherence of this in-between liberalism is beyond the scope of this book, though it is worth noting that the rapid decline and eventual demise of the Liberal Party starting around 1910 shows the difficulty of this moderate liberalism squeezed between the hammer of revolutionary socialism on the left and the anvil of reactionary conservatism on the right. In the particular case of Churchill, it is telling that when his rapidly declining Liberal Party decided to try to save itself by throwing in its lot with the rising socialist Labour Party in the early 1920s, Churchill returned to the Conservative Party. The historian A.J.P. Taylor concluded about the whole of Churchill's career that "he was essentially conservative." Robert Rhodes James concurs, stating that even during his so-called "radical" phase, "Churchill's basic conservatism was a conspicuous feature of his political attitudes."[15]

WHILE REAGAN AND Churchill were both essentially conservative for their entire lives, they exhibited a dislike of political labels—both partisan labels and ideological labels. Each man affected a studied independence from his party for a long time, and used similar rhetoric to describe his attitude about partisanship. Early in his political career, Churchill talked often of trying to form a "party of the center," and when he stood for Parliament again after leaving the Liberal Party in 1924, he ran not under the Conservative Party label but as a self-described "independent constitutionalist." At the end of World War II in Europe, Churchill wanted to continue as head of an all-party coalition government, but the Labour Party demanded an election. In the campaign that followed, Churchill clung to the sentiment of an all-party government, and despite his stinging attacks on the Labour Party he insisted on describing himself as both a Conservative Party candidate and a National candidate, in an attempt to transcend partisanship.

Reagan also displayed an aloofness from political parties. When Reagan ran for governor in 1966, Lou Cannon noticed, "he almost never used the words 'Republican' or 'conservative' in his speeches."[16] In Reagan's case this can be seen as a tactical necessity in a state where Democrats vastly outnumbered Republicans. Yet in his "Time for Choosing" speech in 1964, Reagan tempered his attacks on liberals and liberalism with the trope, "It seems impossible to legitimately debate the issues of the day without being subjected to name-calling and the application of labels. . . . Today we are told that we must choose between left and right, or as others suggest, a third alternative, a kind of safe middle ground. *I suggest to you there is no left or right, only an up or down* [emphasis added]."

In the aftermath of the Watergate scandal, when the Republican Party's popularity was at an all-time low with voters (as few as 18 percent identified themselves as Republicans in polls taken in late 1974), Reagan briefly entertained advice from prominent conservatives to start a new third party. When a reporter asked about the idea, Reagan left the door open: "There could be one of those moments in time, I don't know. I see statements of disaffection of people in both parties." Reagan quickly rejected the idea, however, recognizing that he would do better to remain in the Republican Party: "Is it a third party we need, or is it a new and revitalized second party, raising a banner of no pale pastels, but bold colors which makes it unmistakably clear where we stand on all of the issues troubling the people? Americans are hungry to feel once again a sense of mission and greatness." (This comment finds a rough analogue in a Churchill campaign speech from 1945, in which he admonished his Conservative Party colleagues that it was "no time for windy platitudes and glittering advertisements. The Conservative Party had far better go down telling the truth and acting in accordance with the verities of our position than gain a span of shabbily-bought office by easy and fickle froth and chatter.")[17]

Reagan deliberately began speaking of the need for a "New Republican Party," sounding very much like Churchill in his appeals for a broad-based party: "The New Republican Party I envision will not, and cannot, be limited to the country club big business image that, for reasons both fair and unfair, it is burdened with today. The New Republican Party I am speaking about is going to have room for the man and woman in the factories, for the farmer, for the cop on the beat, and the millions of Americans who may never have thought of joining our party before, but whose interests coincide with those represented by principled Republicanism."[18] Reagan consistently cited poll numbers to show that a majority of Americans agreed with his views, suggesting that his conservatism was the new mainstream.

This studied distance from straight partisanship is another example of both Reagan's and Churchill's independence of mind, and how they did not fit easily into the established categories of partisan thought. In a famous essay on Churchill ("Winston Churchill in 1940"), Isaiah Berlin offered a diagnosis of this problem that applies equally to Reagan: "No strongly centralized political organization feels altogether happy with individuals who combine independence, a free imagination, and a formidable strength of character with stubborn faith and a single-minded, unchanging view of the public and private good."

THEIR CRITICS ASSUMED their idiosyncrasies and unconventional thought owed to a rigid ideological core. This view is mistaken. Both men rejected ideology in forceful terms. To be sure, in *The Gathering Storm* Churchill wrote, "Those who are possessed of a definite body of doctrine and of deeply rooted convictions upon it will be in a much better position to deal with the shifts and surprises of daily affairs." But a few sentences later Churchill acknowledges that "it is always more easy to discover and proclaim general principles than to apply them."[19] In Churchill's thoughts and deeds we see an example of the classical virtue of prudence, the adjustment of principles to circumstances but always with the same dominant purpose in mind.

Reagan offered some extended thoughts on this problem of ideology versus circumstance. In a 1977 speech, Reagan said:

> I have always been puzzled by the inability of some political and media types to understand exactly what is meant by adherence to political principle. All too often in the press and the television evening news it is treated as a call for "ideological purity." Whatever ideology may mean—and it seems to mean a variety of things, depending upon who is using it—it always conjures up in my mind a picture of a rigid, irrational clinging to abstract theory in the face of reality. We have to recognize that in this country "ideology" is a scare word. And, for good reason. Marxist-Leninism is, to give but one example, an ideology. If the facts don't happen to fit the ideology, the facts are chopped off and discarded. I consider this to be the complete opposite to principled conservatism. If there is any political viewpoint in this world which is free of slavish adherence to abstraction, it is American conservatism.[20]

Reagan's Democratic adversary Tip O'Neill once remarked that he hated negotiating with Reagan because Reagan always got 80 percent of what he wanted. Reagan could be confident of compromising when the result moved policy in his direction. The exception that proves the rule was the tax increase Reagan agreed to in 1982. He thought it a principled compromise because the deal called for $3 in reduced spending for every $1 in new taxes; the compromise would result in smaller government, Reagan's dominant purpose. The taxes came in, but Congress never delivered the promised spending cuts. Reagan later listed the deal as one of his biggest mistakes.

Practical people are usually conventional in their thinking. Thus one of the difficulties of understanding Churchill and Reagan is the combination of practical sense alongside unconventional and sometimes outlandish ideas that seemed to be derived purely from ideology. The best many could do in the case of Reagan is to say that he had a pragmatic side and an ideological side (in the words of his chief of staff James Baker, Lou Cannon, and many others) and leave it unresolved. The flywheel that harmonized these incompatible traits remained imperceptible even to Reagan's intimates. Cannon simply concluded that "the whole of Reagan's performance was greater than the sum of its parts." Even such an astute observer as Henry Kissinger described Reagan's performance in office as "astonishing" and "nearly incomprehensible." The most incredulous summation came from one of Reagan's national security advisers, Robert McFarlane, who said, "He knows so little, and accomplishes so much."

As we have come to learn, Reagan knew more than he let on—often much more—but concealed or disguised what he knew for obscure reasons.[21] Churchill never concealed or disguised what he knew. Quite the opposite: he usually seemed at pains to establish himself as the most knowledgeable person in the room. This contrast in their styles of thought and action suggest that *what* they knew was more important than how they knew it, or how they used it. The similarity in their particular political opinions, and how they departed from the conventional conservative thinking of their time, is the subject of the next two chapters.

CHAPTER 7

Churchill and Reagan on Domestic Policy

The inherent vice of Capitalism is the unequal sharing of blessings. The inherent virtue of Socialism is the equal sharing of miseries.

— WINSTON CHURCHILL, 1945

If a Martian spaceship should circle the world looking for the best planned economy they would pick the one that wasn't planned—our own.

— RONALD REAGAN, 1976

As we have seen, Churchill was one of the architects of the modern British welfare state, and Reagan was an admirer of the New Deal's purposes. Both men saw government social insurance serving a conservative function, which made it easy for them to set limits on how extensive public aid should be. Their departure from modern welfare state mentality can be seen in a common phrase that Churchill may have originated and Reagan revived. When Reagan took office in 1981, he pledged that his domestic budget cuts would preserve the "safety net" of programs for those who, "through no fault of their own, must depend on the rest of us—the poverty stricken, the disabled, the elderly, all those in true need." This was uncommon language. A computer text search of the presidential papers stretching back more than fifty years to Herbert Hoover shows the term "safety net" had been used less than a dozen times. Reagan used the term more than seventy times during his presidency.

Liberals hated the term "safety net," and it received derisive treatment in the news media. No one recalled that it was also Churchill's language. Throughout his first decade in domestic cabinet posts from 1906 to 1911, Churchill said the purpose of new social insurance programs was "to spread a net over the abyss." Alternately, he would refer to "the meshes of our safety net." By linking the safety net with the idea of the "truly needy," Reagan was reviving the traditional distinction between the deserving and undeserving poor. This was anathema to liberals. In the 1960s and 1970s the relentless egalitarianism of modern liberalism sought to transform benevolent public assistance into a right. The point was not the adequacy or inadequacy of the safety net but the concept itself. Welfare in liberal dogma was primary about redistribution, not amelioration. Reagan had long resisted the entitlement mentality of modern liberalism. "I believe that the government is supposed to *promote* the general welfare," Reagan said in a TV debate on welfare in 1970; "I don't think it is supposed to *provide* it."[1] This is not far from William Manchester's description of Churchill's attitude toward the modern welfare state: "He wasn't opposed to the substance of Labour's bills; what he found objectionable was the *way* the thing was being done. Labour held that the people had an absolute right to these comprehensive benefits. Churchill thought they should be gifts from a benign upper class to grateful lower classes."[2]

Reagan further infuriated the Left when he argued for a greater role on the part of private charity in alleviating poverty. In 1982 Reagan said that if every church in America were to look after the needs of ten poor families, "we could eliminate all government welfare in this country," and "the actual help would be greater because it would come from the heart."[3] Once again he closely tracks Churchill, who said in 1901, "I object on principle to doing by legislation what properly belongs to charity."

This is merely the beginning of Reagan and Churchill's congruity over domestic social and economic policy. While both supported limited welfare state measures as a "safety net," both understood the moral hazard of benefits that were either too generous or came to be regarded as an entitlement. Churchill noted, "There can be no doubt that the present system of extended unemployment benefit hampers what is called the mobility of labor."[4] Reagan, closely following the research findings of numerous economists, opposed proposals to increase the minimum wage because it would worsen unemployment, especially among minority youth, and wondered aloud several times whether unemployment insurance and other welfare programs *increased* the unemployment rate. "Tax free benefits lure people to quit jobs more frequently [than] they actually lure people into the job market," Reagan said. "The effect is an artificial layer of unemployed who don't reflect the economic situation of the country at all."[5]

Both were adamantly opposed to using deficit spending to stimulate employment during recessions. In 1929, as the Great Depression was beginning to unfold, Churchill, serving as chancellor of the exchequer, opposed a proposal from fellow cabinet members for a government-funded jobs program. John Maynard Keynes had just coauthored a book, *We Can*

Conquer Unemployment, advocating deficit spending to stimulate the economy—a prelude to his *General Theory of Employment, Interest, and Money,* which lent his name to the
convenient new doctrine that justified vastly higher government spending.

Churchill's argument against the jobs scheme anticipated
all the conservative criticisms that would be directed against
Keynesian-style spending programs for the next fifty years.
Churchill made the "crowding out" argument: government
borrowing would compete with private sector borrowing, driv-
ing up interest rates and producing a lower rate of return. In a
long speech in the House of Commons, Churchill noted that
the government already borrowed money for necessary public
works projects, but that "for the purposes of curing unemployment the results have certainly been meager. They are, in fact,
so meager as to lend considerable color to the orthodox
Treasury doctrine which has steadfastly held that, whatever
might be the political or social advantages, very little additional employment and no permanent additional employment
can in fact and as a general rule be created by State borrowing
and State expenditure."[6] Central to Churchill's position was
his view that the private sector invested more intelligently
than the public sector. As Robert Rhodes James observed,
"Belief in private enterprise lay at the core of his being." This
view was far from widespread at that time; not only was socialism considered the wave of the future, but the belief that the
public sector could invest more intelligently than the private
sector was a popular idea.

Churchill prevailed in this fight. The Conservatives who
had wanted the jobs program did so primarily out of fear of
losing the next election. "It is to be hoped," Churchill had
written in a memorandum, "that we shall not let ourselves be

drawn by panic or electioneering into unsound schemes to cure unemployment, and divert national credit from the fertile channels of private enterprise to State undertakings fomented mainly for political purposes."[7] Six weeks later, the Conservative Party was thrown out of office in a general election. (By the mid-1930s, Churchill relented in his opposition to deficit spending and Keynesian stimulus programs.)

Calls for deficit-financed government jobs programs reached a crescendo in the United States in the 1970s, during the period of slow growth and high inflation that came to be known as "stagflation." Labor unions demanded a $100 billion jobs program, at a time when the federal deficit was already nearing $70 billion. Another proposal, the Humphrey-Hawkins bill, would guarantee the right to a job for every American who demanded one. Reagan opposed both ideas. In a series of radio addresses, he made the same argument as Churchill: by running a deficit the government is taking money away from more productive private sector investment. A higher deficit will contribute to higher inflation, and will result in worse unemployment down the road. Like Churchill, Reagan pointed to a disappointing record of previous jobs programs: "In our experience so far with these emergency public jobs programs we've learned that they actually decrease employment because in many instances government entities only use the program to hire those they already intended to hire."[8]

THIS WAS NOT the end of Reagan's or Churchill's critique of the welfare state, however. Both men took their criticism much further than any other prominent conservative figure of their time. Reagan, for example, went on to say, "But there is much, much more to fear in Humphrey-Hawkins. Actually it follows a pattern once used in Italy by a fellow named Mussolini, and then it was called Fascism." This was not Reagan's only invocation of this incendiary term. During the 1976 campaign, Reagan remarked to *Time* magazine that "Fascism was really the basis for the New Deal." Democrats remembered this in the 1980 campaign and attempted to use it against him. Ted Kennedy attacked this remark in his speech to the 1980 Democratic convention, and the media took up the issue. "Those Old Reaganisms May Be Brought Back to Haunt Him," read a *Washington Post* headline about Reagan's "Fascism" remarks. Reagan did not backpedal; to the contrary, he stoutly defended his comment. In late August Reagan told reporters, "Anyone who wants to look at the writings of the Brain Trust of the New Deal will find that President Roosevelt's advisers admired the fascist system. . . . They thought that private ownership with government management and control *à la* the Italian system was the way to go, and that has been evident in all their writings." This was, Reagan added, "long before Fascism became a dirty word in the lexicon of the liberals." The *Washington Post,* among others, was agog: "Several historians of the New Deal period questioned by the *Washington Post* said they had no idea what Reagan was referring to."[9]

Once again Reagan was on to something. To be sure, such a comment was politically imprudent, and is also dissonant with Reagan's favorable evocation of Roosevelt's legacy at other moments in his campaign. To most people fascism means storm troopers, dictators with funny uniforms, and persecution of minorities. Reagan meant it in the precise sense of political economy: public control of private resources.[10] Is Reagan's view wholly outlandish? The economic coordination functions of the National Recovery Administration partook of Reagan's definition of fascism; that the Supreme Court ruled so many of these forms of economic planning to be unconstitutional—in cases that still stand as precedent today—should suggest that Reagan's view, while unconventional, was not entirely nonsensical.

Where did Reagan get it? The most likely source was a book well known to Reagan, F. A. Hayek's *The Road to Serfdom*. There Hayek noted, "Indeed, there is scarcely a leaf out of Hitler's book which somebody or other in England and America has not recommended us to take and use for our own purposes. . . . In 1934 the newly established National Planning Board devoted a good deal of attention to the example of planning provided by these four countries: Germany, Italy, Russia, and Japan."[11] With Reagan's phenomenal memory and vivid imagination, this may have been the only reference Reagan needed to stimulate the remark.

The Hayek influence also shows up in Churchill's comments. In the election campaign held right after the end of the war in Europe, Churchill attacked the Labour Party's socialist agenda with the argument that "no Socialist system can be established without a political police. Many of those who are advocating Socialism or voting Socialist today will be horrified at this idea. That is because they are short-sighted, that is because they do not see where their theories are leading them." Churchill might have been fine if he had stopped here. But he went on to lay out explicitly where socialist theories would lead: "some form of Gestapo," which would "gather all the power to the supreme party and the party leaders, rising like stately pinnacles above their vast bureaucracies of Civil servants, no longer servants and no longer civil."[12] Churchill made this speech on the BBC, and his invocation of the term "Gestapo" in connection with his former coalition partners from the Labour Party went down very badly with British

voters. Churchill's wife and several close colleagues had urged
him to remove the Gestapo reference, but he refused. It ranks
alongside Barry Goldwater's "extremism in defense of liberty"
comment in 1964 as an example of counterproductive rhetoric.[13] Churchill's party lost the 1945 election in a landslide.

Like Reagan, Churchill drew his inspiration for this remark from Hayek, whose description in *The Road to Serfdom* of
how socialism had undermined parliamentary democracy in
Europe resonated with Churchill. *The Road to Serfdom* had
been published with surprising success in 1944, and Churchill
either read or acquired the gist of it (perhaps he saw the
Reader's Digest condensation of the book). Hayek himself later
wrote to Paul Addison, "I am afraid there can be little doubt
that Winston Churchill's somewhat unfortunately phrased
Gestapo speech was written under the influence of *The Road
to Serfdom.*" Churchill met Hayek briefly a few years later, indi-
cated his familiarity with Hayek's book, but told Hayek "it
would never happen in England."[14]

If Churchill is guilty of overextending Hayek's argument
in *The Road to Serfdom* (in later books Hayek allowed as how
the robust traditions of liberty in England probably made the
nation immune to the worst tendencies of socialist despotism), he showed a more acute grasp of one of Hayek's central
contributions to economics: the analysis of how dispersed
knowledge and decision-making in markets will always out-
perform centralized economic planning. As far back as 1908
Churchill anticipated in broad strokes what Hayek would explain more fully in his classic 1945 essay "The Use of
Knowledge in Society." As Churchill put it:

> I reject as impracticable the insane Socialist idea
> that we could have a system whereby the whole na-

tional production of the country, with all its infinite ramifications, should be organized and directed by a permanent official, however able, from some central office. The idea is not only impossible, but unthinkable. If it was even attempted it would produce a most terrible shrinkage and destruction of productive energy.[15]

Many biographies of Churchill suggest that he grew less confident in his economic views in the aftermath of his mixed experience as chancellor of the exchequer from 1925 to 1929. Although he did reverse his views on the gold standard and express some doubts about the ability of Parliament to master economic policy, he never wavered in his mature opposition to socialism. Indeed, in 1929 Churchill contemplated writing a book on socialism to be called *The Creed of Failure.* He went as far as to outline the first five chapters, but abandoned the project when his publishers were unenthusiastic.

It was more than merely economic inefficiency that alienated Churchill and Reagan from socialism. Both had an instinctive resistance to the premises of centralized administration that lay behind not just socialism but all ambitious schemes of active government management of social affairs. American progressivism directly taught that increasing spheres of public life should be removed from the vagaries of party politics and placed in the care of expert administrators—a phenomenon sometimes called "the administrative state." Reagan repeatedly criticized this long-term trend in American government. In his first inaugural address as president in 1981, Reagan put the point in Jeffersonian terms: "From time to time, we have been tempted to believe that society has become too complex to be managed by self-rule, that government by an elite group is superior to government for, by, and of the people. But if no one among us is capable of governing himself, then who among us has the capacity to govern someone else?" (Jefferson had asked in his first inaugural address in 1801, "Sometimes it is said that man can not be trusted with the government of himself. Can he, then, be trusted with the government of others? Or have we found angels in the forms of kings to govern him? Let history answer this question.")

Churchill expressed similar doubts about the administrative state: "On many occasions in the past," Churchill said in 1945, "we have seen attempts to rule the world by experts of one kind or another. There have been the theocratic, the military, and the aristocratic and it is now suggested that we should have scientific—governments."[16] In the infamous "Gestapo" speech, Churchill singled out for criticism the administrative innovation that is known in the United States as "delegation": "Have we not heard Mr. Herbert Morrison descant upon his plans to curtail Parliamentary procedure and pass laws simply by resolution of broad principle in the House of Commons, afterwards to be left by Parliament to the executive and to the bureaucrats to elaborate and enforce by departmental regulations?" Reagan objected to the same dynamic in American government, writing in a 1979 personal letter, "The permanent structure of our government with its power to pass regulations has eroded if not in effect repealed portions of our Constitution."[17]

AN ENTIRELY OVERLOOKED similarity between Churchill and Reagan concerns their attitudes toward income tax policy. Reagan held conventional antitax views, and liked to quote Churchill's similar sentiments, such as Churchill's remark that "the idea that a nation can tax itself into prosperity is one of the crudest delusions which has ever befuddled the human mind." However, it turns out that both men's views on taxes went beyond a mere antistatist dislike. Reagan came to the presidency as a champion of "supply-side economics," and successfully cut income tax rates twice.[18] In two words, supply-side economics simply means "taxes matter." Taxes matter to each individual decision to save, invest, produce, or consume. And the sum of individual decisions adds up to whether the economy is robust or stagnating. Reagan usually explained it in simple terms of incentives: too high tax rates diminished the incentive for investment and work. The Washington establishment considered Reagan a radical revolutionary for proposing to cure a bad economy with large tax cuts. Reagan argued that, to the contrary, the idea had a long pedigree. He delighted in quoting John F. Kennedy and Calvin Coolidge, both of whom cut income tax rates for supply-side reasons.

But Reagan could just have well quoted Churchill.

When Churchill became chancellor of the exchequer in 1925, one of his first proposals was a cut in the "Super-tax," which were high tax rates enacted on upper-income individuals during World War I. (The United States had imposed a similar surtax on the wealthy; it was this surtax that Calvin Coolidge cut first during his presidency at the same time Churchill was cutting rates in England.) Churchill did not claim, as some supply-siders did in the early 1980s, that income tax cuts would generate an increase in revenue, but he did speak in clear tones about incentives and economic growth. "I believe that the Super-tax at its present rate constitutes an excessive burden both on enterprise and on the saving power of the nation," he said in his first budget speech in the House of Commons, "and that it is an impediment to the creation of that new wealth without which our present load of debt and expenditure cannot be borne."[19] Although Keynesianism had not yet become the dominant doctrine, Labour Party figures argued there was no connection between tax rates and economic performance. Churchill argued, as Reagan would argue when his tax cuts came under attack, that tax cuts needed a period of years to work:

> I believe most firmly that the rate of direct taxation upon income was producing a chill and a check upon the enterprise and upon the conceiving energy of the country to an extent certainly far higher than in any other country in the world, and far more heavy in its effect than in any other country in the world. Yet this country, where direct taxation has reached unprecedented and unparalleled dimensions, is also, we find, the country where, at the other end of the social scale, this extraordinary phenomenon of unemployment has manifested itself in the most distressing form. It is said by some that there is no connection between the two. The theory of the hon. Gentlemen opposite is that, the more taxes you pile upon wealth, the greater the benefit to the working classes. Our theory is exactly the opposite, and we are prepared to confront you, not only with continuous argument on that subject, but we hope, having three or four years of power and authority, to confront you with the proved results of the opposite theory.[20]

Like Reagan, Churchill pointed to the positive results of past tax cuts:

The hon. Gentleman spoke about the relation of the rate of Income Tax to unemployment. He said, "How foolish it is to imagine that by reducing Income Tax you improve employment." The fact, however, is that the country with the highest rate of direct taxation is also the country with the highest unemployment. That is the fact. It may be a coincidence. But when the Income Tax was reduced by 1 shilling and then by 6d., there was a great improvement. When the Income Tax was 6 shillings in the Pound there were over 2¼ million persons unemployed. Now that the Income Tax has been reduced to 4 shillings 6d. in the Pound that figure has fallen to 1¼ million people unemployed.

Just as John F. Kennedy justified income tax cuts in the basis that "a rising tide lifts all boats" (a phrase Reagan delighted in taunting Democrats with), Churchill argued that income tax cuts would benefit everyone, not just the rich: "I think, in the time at our disposal, we shall succeed in establishing the soundness of the grounds on which we have acted, and the results which will be effected in the general life of the country by three or four years of steady policy from one broad point of view will be sensibly appreciated by all classes in the State." Like Reagan, he also argued that income tax cuts were justified because inflation had eroded real incomes: "Quite apart from the increase in the rates of taxation, it is levied on an income which purchases not much more than half what it would have purchased before the War. . . . The burden of the Income Tax on the graduated scale has been nearly doubled by the fact that the nominal value of money has so greatly changed."[21] Churchill's opponents charged that his fiscal policy amounted to "a rich man's budget," the exact phrase Reagan's opponents used against him. Churchill complained that this was "gross misrepresentation, dishonest misrepresentation." Reagan made the same protest.

While the policies of Reagan and Churchill are commonly thought to have been pro-business, they both expressed a surprising disdain for the mighty corridors of finance. When financial leaders questioned the soundness of his economic policies—including his tax cuts—Churchill replied, "I would rather see Finance less proud and Industry more content."[22] When Wall Street expressed misgivings about Reagan's economic proposals in the spring of 1981, Reagan dismissed them with the terse one-sentence comment "I have never found Wall Street a source of good economic advice. . . . I think they are looking through a very narrow glass."[23] Heresy for a Republican!

ONE LAST COMMON aspect of Churchill and Reagan that deserves mention is their relationship with organized labor. Both Reagan and Churchill had been union members; in Reagan's case, he is the only American president who had been a union member. Reagan was head of the Screen Actors Guild, an AFL-CIO affiliate, during his Hollywood days, and led contract negotiations with the major Hollywood studios at a time when the film industry was much more concentrated and centralized than it is today. In his 1980 campaign, Reagan explicitly appealed to union voters with the slogan "Elect a former union president, President," and he would sometimes as president hold up his union card when speaking to labor audiences, as he did on March 31, 1981, the day he was shot after having spoken to the AFL-CIO's Building and Construction Trades Conference at the Washington Hilton.

"I'm the first President of the United States to hold a lifetime membership in an AFL-CIO union," he boasted. For a Republican, Reagan received a disproportionate share of union votes in his two runs for president.

Churchill's labor connection was more honorary than substantive. He was a member of the local chapter of the Amalgamated Union of Building Trade Workers, who had invited Churchill in 1928 to join in honor of his bricklaying work at Chartwell. Churchill knew that labor union leaders disliked him, and replied to the invitation, "I should be very pleased to join your union if you are of the opinion that it would not be unwelcome to your members." The executive committee later ruled that Churchill was ineligible, but he had already paid his dues and received his membership card.[24]

Organized labor in Britain regarded Churchill as a bitter enemy, though this reputation was unfair. (An important exception to labor enmity toward Churchill proves this point: When Prime Minister Neville Chamberlain decided in May 1940 that an all-party government of national unity was necessary to carry on the war against Hitler, the Labour Party sent word that Churchill was the only Conservative under whose leadership they would agree to serve.) During his brief but eventful tenure as a young Liberal Party minister with domestic portfolios in the cabinet from 1908 to 1911, Churchill was the prime mover behind a number of social initiatives to benefit the working classes and labor unions. As president of the Board of Trade from 1908 to 1910 (analogous to our secretary of commerce and secretary of labor), Churchill promoted the idea of a Standing Court of Arbitration to resolve industrial disputes, which soon proved their worth in settling unrest in the shoe manufacturing trade, and in the coal, copper, and iron mining industries. He also helped create "labor exchanges" to assist labor mobility (this was in the days before "help wanted" ads in the newspapers[25]) and supported the establishment of a minimum wage and legislation regulating the working conditions of sweatshops. Moreover, Churchill publicly supported union membership—for example, stating in Parliament, "I consider that every workman is well advised to join a trade union. I cannot conceive how any man standing undefended against the powers that be in this world could be so foolish, if he can possibly spare the money from the maintenance of his family, not to associate himself with an organization to protect the rights and interests of labor."[26] For these and related measures in other fields, such as old-age pensions and unemployment insurance, Churchill rightly claimed to have been one of the architects of the modern British welfare state. He took the side of striking miners against mine owners on more than one occasion.

Such a record should put one in good stead with organized labor, but, as with Reagan, Churchill's involvement with several labor controversies erased the goodwill of his positive deeds. The most significant was the infamous coal miners' strike at Tonypandy in 1910. In these early years of organized labor in Britain (as in the United States), strikes often turned violent, so when the Tonypandy miners went out, Churchill, then serving as home secretary, ordered the army to the region as a precaution against an outbreak of rioting. The local police chief, fearing the strikers would overmatch his modest cops, had requested military help from London. Churchill stipulated that military forces be held in reserve for the worst case; in fact they were never used. However, this hint of force, combined with the death of several rioting strikers at the hands of local police and the usual confusion of such episodes, gave rise to the charge that Churchill had ordered the army to fire on strikers. The charge dogged Churchill the rest of his political career. Biographer Norman Rose comments, "The myth of Tonypandy—that, in November 1910, he had ordered the military to fire upon the striking miners of the Rhondda Valley— has no substance in fact. But the legend died hard, disproved but not dispelled. In fact, Churchill acted with admirable restraint in an explosive situation."[27]

An equally controversial chapter in Churchill's labor relations came with the General Strike of 1926. A coal mine lockout quickly grew into a general strike when other unions walked out in sympathy. At the height of the strike, 6 million British workers were off the job, crippling almost all modes of transport and industrial production. The government of Prime Minister Stanley Baldwin took an uncompromising hard line against the strike, with Baldwin depicting the strike as a challenge to the constitution. Churchill, serving in Baldwin's cabinet as chancellor of the exchequer, was said to have been the instigator of Baldwin's tough position, but in fact Churchill was not among the cabinet working group that handled the strike. He did, however, take the lead in running the government newspaper, called *The British Gazette,* which was published because all of London's regular news sheets had been shut down by the strike. Under Churchill's heavy-handed editorial direction, *The British Gazette* was far from an objective or neutral paper. It was a vehicle of propaganda; its pages were belligerently pro-government and depicted the strike as a revolutionary activity. Churchill wrote most of the paper's unsigned editorials himself. By the second week of production, circulation had reached 2.2 million copies.

After the general strike collapsed, labor leaders and leftists turned their ire on Churchill. Churchill is alleged to have said "a little bloodletting" during the strike would be a good thing. Churchill considered suing for libel over the allegation. (If he had said such a thing, it would have offered an analogue for a famous Reagan utterance from 1970, when Governor Reagan, tiring of campus radicalism, let fly with the intemperate remark "If it takes a bloodbath, let's get it over with. No more appeasement.") Even some of Churchill's friends thought he was too harsh in his attitude about the strike. In fact, Churchill had considerable sympathy for the position of the coal miners that had led to the strike, and worked to block or blunt antiunion legislation his Conservative Party wanted to enact. "I am all on the miners' side now," Churchill said after the strike ended. "In a long public life clouded with misunderstandings," William Manchester wrote, "none was more tragic than the inexpiable enmity between Churchill and Labour."[28]

LIKE CHURCHILL, PRESIDENT Reagan came to be regarded as an enemy of labor; in fact, he acquired a reputation as the most antilabor president in modern American history, though this reputation was unfair.[29] Reagan liked to point out that inflation exacts its highest cost on the poor, people with fixed income, and laborers working for fixed contract wages. He never got much credit from organized labor for breaking the back of inflation. His poor reputation with labor stemmed largely from a single incident: his decision to smash a union—the Professional Air Traffic Controllers Organization (PATCO). The irony of the case is that PATCO was one of the very few labor organizations to endorse Reagan in 1980, which led the union leadership to expect sympathetic treatment from him if pressed for large raises in the spring of 1981. Reagan had expressed some sympathy with the union's concerns about working conditions and salary levels, writing to the union that he would address issues such as "too few people working un-reasonable hours with obsolete equipment," which "placed the nation's air travelers in unwarranted danger." If elected, Reagan promised, "I will take whatever steps are necessary to provide our air traffic controllers with the most modern equipment available and to adjust staff levels and work days." Above all, Reagan pledged "a spirit of cooperation" with the union.

But the union came in with unreasonable demands, start-ing with a 100 percent pay increase (at a time when Reagan had frozen federal salaries across the board), a reduction of the workweek to 32 hours, and more than ninety other de-mands. The total cost of PATCO's wish list was estimated at $1.1 billion in the first year alone. "Most Americans regarded the union's demands as ridiculous," *Time* magazine writer William A. Henry observed. Nevertheless, PATCO president Robert Poli threatened darkly that controllers would strike if their demands were not met.

PATCO thought Reagan would fold up, especially given the vulnerability of air travel to a controllers' work stoppage. Reagan warned that a strike would be illegal and that striking workers could be fired. PATCO leaders thought Reagan was bluffing. They had not done their homework. Had they not pondered that notorious portrait of Reagan's model Calvin Coolidge in the cabinet room, the man who had rocketed to national fame with his declaration against the Boston police strike of 1919: "There is no right to strike against the public safety by anybody, anywhere, at any time"? PATCO also did not note that as governor of California, Reagan had twice stomped strikes by public sector employees, in one case threatening State Water Resources Department employees that they would be fired if they did not return to work within five days (the minimum period under California law that Reagan had to allow). On the fifth day, the striking workers returned to their jobs—without a raise.

The air traffic controllers called Reagan's bluff and walked out in July 29, 1981. At 10:55 A.M., Reagan came out to meet the press in the White House Rose Garden and made good on his threat. Reminding the White House press corps once again that he was the only president to have belonged to a labor union and to have once led a strike, a grim-faced and plainly perturbed Reagan reiterated that public sector strikes were intolerable: "I must tell those who fail to report for duty this morning they are in violation of the law, and if they do not report for work within 48 hours, they have forfeited their jobs and will be terminated." There was more. The Reagan administration hit PATCO with millions of dollars in fines, eating up all of the union's modest funds. (The fines eventually reached $150 million.) The administration also began legal proceedings with the Federal Labor Relations Authority to have PATCO decertified, a process that was accomplished in two months. President Poli eventually resigned from the decimated union and ended his working days selling real estate in Florida.

Smashing the air traffic controllers union has loomed large in populist lore ever since as a "signal" to private sector management that it was now okay to squeeze their own unions, but this is too simple. If Reagan had really wanted to send an antiunion message, he would have proposed to privatize air traffic control rather than replace strikers with new government hires. William Niskanen, a member of Reagan's Council of Economic Advisers, points out that in 1983 the Reagan administration was "scrupulously neutral" toward a systemwide strike against AT&T, which was the largest strike

in thirty-seven years. Generally, polls showed that public esteem for organized labor was at an all-time low by the time of
the PATCO's ill-considered gambit.[30] Labor was getting the
message. A *Wall Street Journal* headline a month later told the
story: "Economic Gloom Cuts Labor Union Demands for Big
1982 Contracts."

In turning on the controllers who had been his erstwhile
supporters in the election, Reagan emulated the manner described by Machiavelli in which Cesare Borgia turned on
Remirro de Orco, his instrument for the pacification of
Romagna, in Chapter 7 of *The Prince*.[31] As Machiavelli put it,
"The ferocity of this spectacle left the people at once satisfied
and stupefied." For the news media, Reagan's handling of the
strike became the opening for a new line of Reagan criticism.
The dominant line of criticism during the budget fight had
been that while Reagan's *policies* might be cruel and uncaring,
he himself was a kindly man. Having wondered earlier
whether Reagan was too "nice," Haynes Johnson now wrote, "A
glimmer of a harsher Reagan emerges. . . . For the first time as
president, he has displayed another, less attractive side.
Firmness is fine in a president; indeed, it is desirable. But
something else came through last week—a harsh, unyielding,
almost vengeful and mean-spirited air of crushing opponents."

Organized labor and the American public certainly got
the message that Reagan was not to be trifled with, but another audience also paid close attention to Reagan's handling
of the strike: the Soviet Politburo. Since taking office, the administration had been looking for an opportunity to demon-
strate in some concrete way its toughness toward the Soviet
Union. As is often the case, the most effective opportunity
came in an unanticipated way and from an unexpected place.
The White House realized it had gotten Moscow's attention

when the Soviet "news" agency TASS decried Reagan's "brutal repression" of the air traffic controllers.

It took several years before Soviet leaders finally sat down face-to-face with Reagan, but when they did, they were as surprised by what happened as their predecessors had been at Churchill's sudden embrace during World War II. Before long, of course, Reagan had helped set in motion processes that did to the Soviet Union what he had done to the air traffic controllers.

CHAPTER 8

From Fulton to Berlin: The Connecting Thread of the Cold War

What do you suppose would be the position this after-noon had it been Communist Russia instead of free enter-prise America which had created the atomic weapon? Instead of being a somber guarantee of peace it would have become an irresistible method of human enslave-ment.

— WINSTON CHURCHILL, 1948

At the end of World War II, one nation in the world had unprecedented power. . . . We had the atomic bomb, that great weapon. . . . The United States made no effort to impose its will on the rest of the nations. Can you hon-estly say that had the Soviet Union been in a comparable position with that bomb, or today's Red Chinese, that the world would not today have been conquered with that force?

— RONALD REAGAN, 1967

WE COME at last to the Cold War, where the paral-lels between Churchill and Reagan are the deep-est. Here we see the political virtue of practical judgment worked out at the highest level. Both men thought the Cold War could be ended peacefully, even as most of their contemporaries thought the Cold War was a permanent condition that could only be "managed." Churchill thought he saw a way to do it, but was unable to put his strategy in motion during his lifetime. Reagan adopted Churchill's Cold War strategy, and saw the last days of the Soviet Union. Both knew that a resolution to the Cold War could not be accomplished in a straight line. But at the core of their view was a shared insight that Communism was doomed.

The anti-Communism of both men is legendary, yet both men at decisive moments were able to form cordial working relationships with the leaders of the Soviet Union—Josef Stalin and Mikhail Gorbachev. Churchill and Reagan placed a high value on face-to-face diplomacy, believing that they could make breakthroughs on the force of their own personalities alone. This may appear as naïve or overconfident—a source of weakness—yet it worked out, arguably better in Reagan's case. Anticipating postwar difficulty in 1944, Churchill said that if he could dine with Stalin once a week, "there would be no trouble at all." Along with Churchill's repeated axioms about strength and appeasement, he also thought conflicts could be resolved through "individual sentiment and human affection." Repeatedly over the years, Reagan expressed the view that he could resolve the Cold War if he could just sit down with his Soviet counterpart and discuss matters rationally. (He admitted that the Soviet leader would need to understand the futility of the arms race and Communist ideology, and that "to be candid, I doubted I'd ever meet anybody like that.") Churchill occasionally observed that the Russians feared our friendship as much as our enmity. Reagan would say that the Soviets feared Western freedom, but that if he could just get

Gorbachev into a helicopter or airplane simply to fly over the United States and "get through to him about the difference between our two systems, I really think we could see big changes in the Soviet Union."[1] Even Reagan's admirers thought him hopelessly naïve about this.

The Soviet Union had no greater antagonist at its birth than Winston Churchill. Expressing his hatred of Communism taxed his extraordinary vocabulary for the rest of his life. Communism was a "pestilence," a "loathsome moral disease," "the poison peril from the east." "Of all tyrannies in history," he said in 1919, "the Bolshevik tyranny is the worst, the most destructive, and the most degrading." It was Churchill who originated the phrase describing the German transport of Lenin from Switzerland to Russia: "in a sealed truck like a plague bacillus."[2] Lenin's hatreds, Churchill wrote, were "tight as a hangman's noose."

As secretary of state for war in the early years after World War I, Churchill tried to strangle Bolshevism in its cradle, sending arms to aid the White Russian resistance, and at one point advocating direct British intervention. Churchill had little support for this effort; Prime Minister Lloyd George deprecated it as "a purely mad enterprise." It ended ignominiously, and became another item in the bill of particulars against Churchill's judgment. Martin Gilbert wrote, "The end of intervention left Churchill personally embittered, and even more distrusted than before. . . . And in the public mind it was yet further proof that he was a man who delighted in war."[3] "The country," Sir William Sutherland wrote, "regard him as a bold, bad man."

After his efforts to stamp out the infant Soviet nation failed, Churchill continued his forceful denunciations. In 1929 he lamented, "Russia, self-outcast, sharpens her bayonets in her Arctic night, and mechanically proclaims through self-starved lips her philosophy of hatred and death."[4] In *Thoughts and Adventures* he elaborated, "There is not one single social or economic principle or concept in the philosophy of the Russian Bolshevik which has not been realized, carried into action, and enshrined in immutable laws a million years ago by the White Ant."[5]

The most remarkable and intriguing aspect of Churchill's and Reagan's anti-Communism is that both men believed that Communism would come to an end someday. This departed from the views of most other anti-Communists, many of whom, like Richard Nixon, thought Soviet Communism was a permanent phenomenon that could only be managed, while Henry Kissinger occasionally voiced fears that Soviet Communism would come to overshadow Western democracy.[6] (This is not to mention the pessimistic Whittaker Chambers, whom Reagan liked to quote, but who wrote that he thought he had joined the losing side when he left the Communist Party.) Churchill said early on that Communism would fail because "it is fundamentally opposed to the needs and dictates of the human heart, and of human nature itself." Later he became more precise in his prediction. In 1952, while Stalin was still alive, Churchill told his young aide John Colville that if he lived his normal span of life he would surely see Eastern Europe free from Communism.[7] (Close: Colville died in 1987.) It is not clear whether Churchill included the Soviet Union itself in this prediction.[8] If pressed, one may guess from his extensive writing about Russia that he might have predicted that Russia would throw off formal Communism and revert to traditional czarist-style authoritarianism, which is what seems to be taking place today.

Reagan's hatred of Communism was just as fervent and

vividly expressed. "I stick pins in a Russian doll every night," Reagan wrote in a private letter in 1983. Like Churchill, Reagan understood the failings of Communism in terms of human nature, calling Marxism "a form of insanity—a temporary aberration which will one day disappear from the earth because it is contrary to human nature." Like Churchill in 1918, Reagan backed up his anti-Soviet words with anti-Soviet deeds, especially his decisions to step up military aid to the anti-Soviet resistance in Afghanistan and elsewhere and to squeeze the Soviet economy through various means. The purpose of his policy was to increase the cost of empire to the Soviet Union, even as he was hoping to sit down with the Soviets to ease tensions.

The inevitable collapse of Communism became an early and persistent theme of his presidency, most notably in his speech to the British Parliament in 1982, when, committing rhetorical larceny, he suggested that it would be Marxism-Leninism that would end up "on the ash heap of history."[9] No president had ever spoken this way about Soviet Communism. Less noticed in that speech was Reagan's invocation of Churchill's most famous Cold War message, the Iron Curtain speech in Fulton, Missouri, in 1946, something he had done several times over the years in his speeches, articles, and radio broadcasts. At Westminster Reagan evoked Churchill's style of thought and rhetoric, and quoted directly from Churchill's Iron Curtain speech:

> Must civilization perish in a hail of fiery atoms? Must freedom wither in a quiet, deadening accommodation with totalitarian evil? Sir Winston Churchill refused to accept the inevitability of war or even that it was imminent. He said, "I do not

believe that Soviet Russia desires war. What they desire are the fruits of war and the indefinite expansion of their power and doctrines. But what we have to consider here today while time remains, is the permanent prevention of war and the establishment of the conditions of freedom and democracy as rapidly as possible in all countries."

The Iron Curtain speech is, like Churchill himself, celebrated today as one of the iconic moments of the Cold War. It is useful to recall, then, the severe criticism the speech received at the time it was given. The criticism was so severe that President Truman disavowed that he had any advance knowledge of the speech, even though he had traveled with Churchill by train and had approved its contents. (Keep in mind that George Kennan's famous "long telegram" from Moscow that promoted the idea of containment had come to the White House just three weeks before Churchill's speech.) The Labour Party government back in London was quick to announce that Churchill was speaking purely as a private citizen.

Media reaction was emphatically negative. Former vice president Henry Wallace, who would challenge Truman in the election two years later, wrote in *The New Republic:* "Few public addresses in the history of the world have been so loaded with dynamite as Churchill's Fulton Iron-Curtain, Anglo-American speech. The American people were shocked and staggered by its content." (*The New Republic* had long been on record disapproving Churchill, editorializing in 1944 that we might as well "expect an African witch doctor to perform a delicate surgical operation as to expect such a man to take the lead in creating a better new world.") Walter Lippmann, who is often credited with originating the term "Cold War" (George Orwell is the term's other putative father), privately called the speech a "catastrophic blunder." A *Christian Century* editorial said, "Not even Hitler in the days of his power resorted to more naked military warnings than Churchill thundered forth in his Missouri speech."

There is a parallel between Churchill's Iron Curtain speech and the high point of Reagan's anti-Soviet rhetoric, which came in his famous 1983 speech before the National Association of Evangelicals in Orlando, Florida. This was the speech in which he called the Soviet Union an "evil empire." Like the Iron Curtain speech, Reagan's "evil empire" speech generated ferocious criticism, perhaps more than any other speech Reagan ever delivered. Historian Henry Steele Commager said, "It was the worst presidential speech in American history, and I've seen them all." *The New Republic* huffed that "the speech left friends and foes around the world with the impression that the President of the United States was contemplating holy war." The *Washington Post*'s Richard Cohen called Reagan a "religious bigot." *New York Times* columnist Anthony Lewis complained that the speech was "outrageous" and "primitive." "What is the world to think," Lewis wrote, "when the greatest of powers is led by a man who applies to the most difficult human problem a simplistic theology?" One remarkable aspect of the reaction is that U.S. critics used harsher language than the Soviets, who merely called the speech "provocative" and "bellicose." The Soviet newspaper *Pravda* made a point of quoting negative Western media reaction, which made it unnecessary for them to tax their own vocabulary.

A few of Reagan's own senior aides privately agreed — communications director David Gergen called the "evil empire" phrase "outrageous"—and had tried to get it removed from the speech. (Another important person who was uneasy with Reagan's tough anti-Soviet rhetoric was his wife, Nancy.) Gergen and others backed down when they discovered that Reagan himself had insisted on including the phrase in the speech and had actually toughened that section of the speech with some flourishes of his own. Reagan was very conscious and deliberate in his choice of language, telling an interviewer a few weeks after the speech, "I made the 'Evil Empire' speech and others like it with malice aforethought."

As with Churchill's Iron Curtain speech, regard for the "evil empire" speech has risen with the passage of time and especially with the demise of the Soviet Union. Soviet dissidents such as Natan Sharansky testified that the "evil empire" speech bolstered their morale: "Finally, the leader of the free world had spoken the truth." Seweryn Bailer, one of the West's leading Sovietologists, and a critic of Reagan, returned from a visit to the Soviet Union shortly after the speech to report that "President Reagan's rhetoric has badly shaken the self-esteem and patriotic pride of the Soviet political elites." A number of former Soviet officials admitted after 1991 that Reagan had been right all along.[10] Even Strobe Talbott, one of Reagan's toughest critics, admitted, "He may have been impolitic, but he was not wrong."[11]

The critics of both speeches, transfixed by the headline-grabbing phrases "Iron Curtain" and "evil empire," did not comprehend the complete arguments that Churchill and Reagan offered. The core of Churchill's argument in Fulton was peace through strength: "From what I have seen of our Russian friends and allies during the war, I am convinced that there is nothing they admire so much as strength, and there is nothing for which they have less respect than weakness, especially military weakness." Churchill added that this made the traditional realpolitik idea of "balance of power" obsolete in an era of nuclear weapons, because a rough balance of power would prove too tempting to the Soviets, especially if Western unity dissolved. This is exactly the situation Reagan warned against in the 1970s, and then had to face as president, when the Soviets made their last throw to split the Western alliance with their installation of short-range nuclear missiles in Eastern Europe and their vigorous political campaign to prevent American countermoves.

Churchill reminded his audience in Fulton of the logic of deterrence and the hazard of appeasement by referring to the experience of the 1930s: "There never was a war in all history easier to prevent by timely action than the one which has just desolated such great areas of the globe. It could have been prevented in my belief without the firing of a single shot." It is obvious from reading Reagan's many speeches and articles on foreign affairs that he had fully absorbed Churchill's logic. In the "evil empire" speech, Reagan offered his own version of Churchill's lesson, which Reagan called "an historical reluctance to see totalitarian powers for what they are. We saw this phenomenon in the 1930s. We see it too often today. . . . If history teaches anything, it teaches that simple-minded appeasement or wishful thinking about our adversaries is folly."

In his drive to the presidency in the late 1970s—a period that might be regarded as Reagan's own "wilderness years"— Reagan draw an explicit parallel between the climate of appeasement in the 1930s and the decay of détente in the 1970s.[12] After President Jimmy Carter announced the completion of the SALT II treaty in 1979, Reagan said, "Heard in the background music to that speech [was] the sorry tapping of Neville Chamberlain's umbrella on the cobblestones of Munich. He, too, talked of peace in our time."[13] Reagan even worried publicly that the Soviet Union could deliver an ultimatum to the United States as early as the next year and "at least by 1981."

Reagan's reference to the parallels with the 1930s caused alarm among some of his political advisers. His campaign strategists were sensitive to the charge that Reagan was a "warmonger." Opinion polls revealed cognitive dissonance among the public on the subject of détente and arms control. About 50 percent of Americans told pollsters that they felt America was slipping behind the Soviets militarily, but more than two-thirds expressed strong support for the arms control process, with 69 percent telling the Harris poll that they favored "the U.S. and Russia seeking areas of agreement and cooperation." Only 42 percent said they favored a "get tough" policy.

Reagan's principal foreign policy adviser, Richard Allen, warned Reagan that "for many, you come across as a 'saber-rattler,' a 'button pusher' or as 'too willing to send in the Marines.' " There needs to be, Allen recommended, *a deliberate attempt to soften the delivery of your message* [emphasis added]."[14] Other advisers shared Allen's concern, suggesting that Reagan tone down his rhetoric and historical analogies to the 1930s. Fred C. Iklé, who had served as head of the Arms Control and Disarmament Agency under President Nixon and was a Reagan adviser, wrote to Peter Hannaford in the spring of 1979 with the "editorial suggestion" that "analogies to the 1930s should be avoided in discussions of our foreign and defense policy addressed to the general public. I fear, to the younger generation, they may either fail to stir up the right associations or appear anachronistic. Even for expert audiences, the many differences between that era and ours tend to provoke unnecessary quibbling."[15] Allen concurred, writing to Hannaford, "In connection with Fred Iklé's suggestion concerning use of the 1930s (especially the Chamberlain line), I am in complete agreement." Reagan ignored their advice.

In addition to the parallels Reagan drew between appeasement in the 1930s and détente in the 1970s, he shared Churchill's logic about arms control. Churchill referred to the enthusiasm for disarmament in the 1930s as "a solemn and prolonged farce," and understood that disarmament did not mean peace. Armaments were a *symptom*, not a *cause*, of international tensions, he maintained, and he repeatedly urged Britain's leaders to look to "the political and economic causes which lie behind the maintenance of armies and navies." "Disarmament has nothing to do with peace," Churchill averred. "When you have peace, you will have disarmament." In the 1970s arms control became the centerpiece of U.S.–Soviet relations and the chief barometer of whether relations were improving. Reagan knew this was a fig leaf, and cited some of the same examples as Churchill, such as the Washington Naval Agreement of 1921. "Do arms limitation agreements—even good ones—really bring or preserve peace?" Reagan asked in 1979. "History would seem to say 'no.' " Reagan liked to say—and did say directly to Gorbachev at their first meeting—that "we do not mistrust each other because we are armed; we are armed because we mistrust each other."

Reagan invoked Churchill's lessons from the 1930s throughout his presidency, often at greater length than in the "evil empire" speech. In his 1982 state-of-the-union speech, Reagan said, "A recognition of what the Soviet empire is about is the starting point. Winston Churchill, in negotiating with the Soviets, observed that they respect only strength and resolve in their dealings with other nations. That's why we've moved to reconstruct our national defenses." In a speech in November 1982, Reagan said:

> Winston Churchill labeled [World War II] the "unnecessary war," because he said there never was a war more easy to stop. And no man had more right to say that than Winston Churchill. He had fought the illusions that led to war, pleaded with his countrymen to recognize and arm against this expanding totalitarian war machine, pleaded with his countrymen to be strong and to have courage—not because he wanted war, but because this was the only way to preserve peace. Yet, for all this, Churchill was castigated as a warmonger.[16]

And then again, a month after the "evil empire" speech:

> A few brave voices tried to warn of the danger. Winston Churchill was driven into the political wilderness for speaking the unpleasant truth. There were also those who in their sincere desire for peace were all too ready to give totalitarians every benefit of the doubt and all too quick to label Churchill a warmonger. Well, time has proven that those who gloss over the brutality of tyrants are no friends of peace or freedom.[17]

BUT CHURCHILL DIDN'T rest his argument on strength alone. "What is needed is a settlement . . . a good understanding on all points with Russia," Churchill said—a statement that was largely overlooked at the time and has been ever since. A favorable settlement with Russia could only be achieved, Churchill thought, under the condition of Western military superiority that existed at that time. The American monopoly of nuclear weapons loomed large in Churchill's mind. He thought the early years after World War II, and as late as the mid-1950s, when American military superiority was still evident, was a propitious time to reach a favorable Cold War settlement. As he warned in Fulton, "the longer this is delayed the more difficult it will be and the greater our dangers will be."

Churchill, in the words of the German scholar Klaus Larres, "became the first practitioner of détente in the postwar world."[18] Churchill was especially hopeful of a negotiated settlement of the Cold War in the immediate aftermath of Stalin's death in 1953, at which time Churchill was prime minister again. But President Eisenhower brusquely rejected Churchill's repeated proposals to arrange a summit with Stalin's uncertain successors. The conventional view is that Churchill overestimated the force of his own personality and the willingness of the Soviets to deal at that moment, but second thoughts are emerging. Historian John Lukacs has written that "perhaps a great chance may have been missed fifty years ago, when Churchill, as so often during his life, was willing to act on his own vision and go against the tide, and when he was right and his opponents were wrong."[19]

It may be just as well that Churchill never got to sit down again with Stalin or his successors during the Cold War, as the momentum of ideological revolutionary fervor virtually assured that the Soviet Union would lurch onward to its "we will bury you" phase of Communist bravado and international intrigue in the 1960s and 1970s. Lukacs wonders whether "that element of romantic sensibility which may be inherent in many instances of a visionary capacity carried Churchill too far" in his dealings with Stalin. At one moment in the 1930s Churchill admitted that, were he forced to choose, he would prefer Nazism to Communism. This judgment did not last long. He soon came to see, earlier than most of his colleagues, that Nazism was the growing threat to Europe, while the Soviet Union, even with its revolutionary doctrine, was contained in the East.

Still, it was a surprise when Churchill embraced Stalin with enthusiasm in 1941 after Hitler attacked the Soviet Union. Churchill immediately took steps to begin sending badly needed supplies to the Soviet Union. Prior to that moment, Churchill had regarded Stalin as "a callous, a crafty, and an un-informed giant." Churchill now said, "If Hitler invaded Hell, I should at least make a favorable mention of the Devil in the House of Commons." He told the House of Commons the day after Hitler launched his attack in the east, "No one has been a more consistent opponent of Communism than I have for the last 25 years. I will unsay no word I have spoken about it. But all this fades away before the spectacle that is now unfolding."

And so Churchill struck up a cordial and at times even warm relationship with Stalin, a dictator whose record of human slaughter surpasses Hitler's. They began exchanging gifts and birthday greetings. Churchill at least once referred to Stalin as "a great and good man," and as late as the Potsdam conference in July 1945 Churchill could still say, "I like that man." Churchill and Stalin had forceful clashes during their private talks, but these clashes of will were offset by long convivial meals followed by hours of drinks and conversation through the small hours of the morning. John Lukacs observes that Churchill "saw Stalin as a national dictator: a brutal and cynical leader *but a statesman nevertheless* [emphasis added]."[20]

Churchill's quick and unqualified alliance with Stalin has been a source of criticism ever since. A few Churchill critics suggest that Churchill missed an opportunity to end the war on decent terms with Germany, and leave the Nazis and the Communists to fight it out between themselves. (In the United States, Senator Harry Truman briefly endorsed this view in 1941, going so far as to suggest that the United States should aid whichever side was losing so as to prolong the fighting.) Of course, as the war proceeded, it became obvious that the Soviet Union would seek to dominate Eastern Europe after the war's end. Its military advance against Germany was not liberation, but conquest. Churchill understood this, but also recognized a fact that eluded his critics: half of Europe free was better than none of Europe free, which would have been the result of abandoning the war against Hitler.[21] As such Churchill's policy was not merely following the old adage "the enemy of my enemy is my friend."

Churchill was always highly skilled at justifying his necessary course reversals (so was Reagan) while affecting a perfect consistency. At the beginning of World War II, Churchill made his famous statement that Russia was "a riddle wrapped in a mystery inside an enigma." The next sentences are usually forgotten: "But perhaps there is a key. That key is Russian national interest." By transforming Stalin from a revolutionary leader into a nationalist leader, Churchill was able to mitigate his own long anti-Communist record.

Unlike Churchill, Reagan never faced the necessity of having to reconcile his hatred of Communism with the necessity of allying with the Soviet Union to avert a greater catastrophe. Thus is it all the more to his credit that he was able to display a Churchillian combination: a deliberate strategy of improving America's relative strength, through a military buildup and an ideological offensive, and the flexibility to await patiently for a breakthrough, which required years of diplomacy and trust-building. Echoing Churchill's sentiments at Fulton, Reagan said early in his presidency, "I've always recognized that ultimately there's got to be a settlement, a solution. The other way, if you don't believe that, then you're trapped in the back of your mind, the inevitability of a conflict some day. . . . That kind of conflict is going to end the world."[22]

Reagan in the 1980s was able to bring to fruition Churchill's design for the 1950s. Many observers still find it hard to believe that the seemingly simpleminded Reagan could have had such a deliberate strategy, one that required a fine balancing between clashing standpoints. Much of his own staff, starting with his first secretary of state, Al Haig, never did grasp his strategy, which is one reason for the bitter factional fights within the foreign policy bureaus of the Reagan administration. During his recovery after being shot in 1981, Reagan sent a handwritten letter to Leonid Brezhnev. Haig and other advisers didn't want Reagan to send it. One reason for their dismay was language such as this: "Is it possible," Reagan asked Brezhnev,

> that we have permitted ideology, political and economic philosophies, and governmental policies to keep us from considering the very real, everyday problems of our peoples? . . . Mr. President, should we not be concerned with eliminating the obstacles which prevent our people from achieving their most cherished goals? And isn't it possible some of these

> obstacles are born of government objectives which
> have little to do with the real need and desires of
> our people?

Despite its Reaganesque sincerity, this is curious language, coming close to validating the revisionist view that the Cold War was an irrational "misunderstanding," perhaps even implying a moral equivalence at some level. Reagan wrote later that he "aimed at reaching [Brezhnev] as a human being." It was the first of several handwritten personal letters Reagan sent to Soviet leaders, all showing the same kind of "romantic sensibility" that can be observed in Churchill.

Yet the same Reagan who tried to appeal on the human level to his Soviet counterpart and who could suggest that Gorbachev might swoon at the sight of a landscape of Wal-Marts and suburban homes was also capable of the clearest and most hardheaded assessments of what had to be done, such as was expressed in a private letter in 1983: "I have never believed in any negotiation with the Soviets that we could appeal to them as we would to people like ourselves." They key is Reagan's tacit distinction between *talking* to the Soviets as people and *negotiating* with the Soviets as an adversary. He continued this letter with a succinct outline of his strategy and policy: "Negotiations with the Soviets is really a case of presenting a choice in which they face alternatives they must consider on the basis of cost. For example in our arms reductions talks they must recognize that failure to meet us on some mutually agreeable level will result in an arms race in which they know they cannot maintain superiority. They must choose between reduced, equal levels or inferiority." Against ferocious criticism at home and nervousness among our allies abroad, Reagan stuck to this strategy even after the Soviet

Union broke off arms control talks in 1983 when the United States installed its first medium-range nuclear missiles in Europe. "They'll be back," Reagan calmly predicted.

Reagan was right. Starting in Geneva in 1985, Reagan began a working relationship with Mikhail Gorbachev that was as unlikely—but equally consequential—as Churchill and Stalin in World War II. Nothing much came of that first meeting beyond a general agreement that the United States and the Soviet Union must get along, but then Reagan didn't expect much from their first meeting. Reagan was alternately combative and genial, going hard after the Soviets in the formal sessions and warming to Gorbachev in their one-on-one sessions. Reagan took a liking to Gorbachev; it took longer for Gorbachev to reciprocate. Just as Stalin had been initially wary of Churchill because of his long anti-Communist record, Gorbachev and his entourage were unsurprised by Reagan's ideological criticisms. "Reagan appeared to me no simple conservative, but a political 'dinosaur,' " Gorbachev recalled in his memoirs.

But they stayed at it, with Reagan sticking to his core point that the United States would win an arms race in the absence of a real arms reduction agreement, and finally in 1987 Gorbachev capitulated to Reagan's original negotiating position, the "zero option," which required removing all intermediate-range nuclear missiles from Europe. It was the first time an entire class of strategic nuclear weapons was eliminated through negotiations, and it paved the way for similar cuts in long-range, intercontinental missiles shortly after. Simultaneously, the Soviet Union began to withdraw from Afghanistan and to relax its control of Eastern Europe, just as Churchill predicted would happen. Standing in Red Square with Gorbachev in 1988, Reagan sensed that the Cold War was all over but the shouting, and declared that the Soviet Union was no longer an "evil empire."

The linchpin of Reagan's negotiating position, and the sticking point at the first two summits with Gorbachev, draws another parallel between Reagan and Churchill. Weeks after the furor over the "evil empire" speech, Reagan took to national television to announce his "strategic defense initiative" (SDI), an ambitious proposal for ballistic missile defense that Reagan thought held out the promise of mitigating or ending the balance of terror posed by nuclear missiles. Most of Reagan's foreign policy team regarded SDI as a "bargaining chip" to be used in arms control negotiations, but Reagan actually believed in the idea, and refused to put the chip in play. When the domestic political attacks on SDI mounted, instead of playing the bargaining chip, Reagan played the Churchill card, as in this remark from 1986:

> You know, before World War II, the British were developing a new defense system; it was called radar. And without radar, it's possible that the Royal Air Force wouldn't have been able to beat back the Nazi air assault on England. If you'll recall—you won't recall, you weren't here at the time, but those of us who do—but you've perhaps read that when Winston Churchill acknowledged what that little band of fighter pilots had done from England, and to save England, and with the help of that radar, when he said, "Never in the course of human events have so many owed so much to so few." Well, I couldn't help but think that giving up SDI would

have been like Chamberlain giving up radar, as well
as Czechoslovakia, at Munich—a tragic blunder that
might have spelled the end to freedom in Europe.[23]

JUST AS THE Churchill-Stalin relationship still raises eye-
brows, a few conservatives in the late 1980s viewed the growing rapport and arms agreements between Reagan and
Gorbachev with alarm. "Some conservatives worry that
Reagan has been beguiled by Gorbachev to the detriment of
American interests," Hedrick Smith reported in the *New York
Times Magazine.* Republican senator James McClure of Idaho
worried, "We've had leaders who got into a personal relationship and have gotten soft—I'm thinking of Roosevelt and
Stalin."[24] If McClure's comment was less than subtle, other
conservatives didn't even try to be artful. Conservative activist
Howard Phillips said Reagan was "fronting as a useful idiot for
Soviet propaganda." There was talk among some conservatives
of founding an "Anti-Appeasement Alliance" to oppose
Reagan's diplomatic overtures to the Soviet Union. These
doubts about Reagan were not limited to the know-nothing
ranks of right-wingers. George Will, Reagan's great friend and
frequent booster, charged that Reagan was engaging in "the
moral disarmament of the West by elevating wishful thinking
to the status of political philosophy."[25]

The best indicator that Reagan was not selling out came
right in the middle of his process of forging a new détente
with the Soviet Union, when he stood before the Berlin
Wall—the most visible and potent symbol of the Iron
Curtain—and demanded that the Soviet Union tear it down.
Reagan's political aides had tried to talk him out of saying
"tear down this wall," because they thought the idea unrealis-
tic and that Reagan would only embarrass himself. The media

snickered that the old Reagan was back, that his speechwriters had gotten to him again. Reagan, the *New York Times* said in its news story, "revived a *long dormant* debate over the Berlin Wall [emphasis added]."[26] "Long dormant" for whom? Certainly not the people of East Germany. In fact, it was Reagan himself who once again overruled his advisers and insisted on keeping the line in his speech. Two years later the Wall was gone, and the Cold War with it. Reagan's Berlin Wall speech stands as a rhetorical bookend with Churchill's Iron Curtain speech. Churchill's speech in Fulton signified the Iron Curtain coming down; Reagan's speech heralded its lifting, and represented the culmination of his rhetorical offensive on behalf of the West.

There is lively debate about whether Reagan himself thought the Soviet Union would collapse so quickly if pressed. Robert Gates, who served as deputy director and later director of the CIA, wrote, "Reagan, nearly alone, truly believed in 1981 that the Soviet system was vulnerable, not in some vague, long-range historical sense, but right then. . . . So he pushed—hard." In response to a sarcastic press question in the fall of 1981, Reagan said, "I think the things we're seeing, not only in Poland but the reports that are beginning to come out of Russia itself about the younger generation and its resistance to longtime government controls, is an indication that communism is an aberration. It's not a normal way of living for human beings, and I think we are seeing the first, beginning cracks, the beginning of the end."

Reagan's critics think he was more lucky than prescient; his view that the Soviet Union could be "transcended" was more a matter of narrow ideology than insight, they maintain, though it is never explained why Reagan (and Churchill), almost alone among conservatives, thought this. Other ob-

servers argue that the credit owes to Gorbachev; *Time* magazine went so far as to name Gorbachev "person of the
decade" in 1990. This is more than a bit precious. Whatever
Gorbachev's qualities and actions, it was surely never part of
his intention to preside over the demise of the Soviet Union
and its ruling Communist Party. Gorbachev himself offers the
ultimate refutation of this view, telling the History Channel in
2002 that "I am not sure what happened would have happened had he [Reagan] not been there."[27]

The final testimony must be Gorbachev's presence at
Reagan's funeral in 2004, where he sat during the formal ser-
vices next to Margaret Thatcher—the person who said of
Gorbachev, "We can do business with this man." If after the
election of 1980 someone had predicted not only that Ronald
Reagan would set in motion the end of the Soviet Union but
that the last leader of the "evil empire" would pay personal
tribute to Reagan at his passing as well, most people would
have looked nervously for the men in the white coats to
intervene.

Churchill would not have been surprised.

CHAPTER 9

Measuring Great Statesmen: Will We See Their Like Again?

The challenge of statesmanship is to have the vision to dream of a better, safer world and the courage, persistence and patience to turn that dream into a reality.

— RONALD REAGAN, 1985

AMONG SOPHISTICATED circles in modern times, we are taught to be embarrassed to speak openly of human greatness. The egalitarian temper, combined with the predilection in the social sciences for emphasizing subrational or material causes for all events and trends, explicitly devalues the role of great individuals in shaping history.

Greatness, especially political greatness, carries a whiff of political incorrectness. This was clearly why *Time* magazine decided against naming Churchill "Person of the Century," even though he had been *Time*'s "Man of the Half-Century" in 1950. At that time the magazine said "no man's history can sum up the dreadful, wonderful years, 1900–1950. Churchill's story comes closest." At century's end *Time* felt compelled to explain why their "Man of the Half-Century" didn't make it for the whole century. "So why is he not Person of the Century?"

159

Time asked. "Well, the passage of time can alter our perspective. A lot has happened since 1950. . . . In his approach to domestic issues, individual rights and the liberties of colonial subjects, Churchill turned out to be a romantic refugee from a previous era who ended up on the wrong side of history."[1]

In place of greatness, today we have mere celebrity, best exemplified by another famous Time-Life publication, *People* magazine. Often we build people up partly to derive pleasure from watching them fall—or be dragged down. Churchill biographer William Manchester took note of this baleful condition and concluded, "If there is a high office in the United States to which Winston Churchill could be elected today, it is unknown to me."

Fortunately, ordinary citizens know better. Although recent British TV documentaries and books on the twentieth century gave slight shrift to Churchill, the British people in a recent poll voted Churchill the greatest Briton in the nation's long, storied history, putting him ahead of Shakespeare.[2] In America the outpouring of sentiment at the time of Reagan's death, in June 2004, made palpable the depth of the nation's regard for him. This astonished the news media, which did its best to diminish Reagan during his presidency. During the week of his passing, CNN's Bernard Shaw admitted that the media had Reagan wrong: "I think we failed our viewers, listeners, and readers to an appreciable extent. . . . The news media failed to thoroughly cover and communicate the very essences we're talking about possessed by Ronald Reagan. . . . I certainly missed a lot." Better late than never, one might say.

At least part of Churchill's enormous ego and self-consciousness of his own greatness derived from his just pride in his practical political ability. Alexander Hamilton wrote that the love of fame is the ruling passion of the noblest minds, and we can see in Churchill that the thirst for personal honor was the spur to perform great and noble deeds. Yet as we saw in Chapter 6, Churchill himself shared some of the modernist doubts about whether the scale of the modern world was narrowing the field for human greatness. "Modern conditions do not lend themselves to the production of the heroic or superdominant type," he wrote in "Mass Effects in Modern Life." In *My Early Life* he posed the question in terms often voiced today: "I wonder often whether any other generation has seen such astounding revolutions of data and values as those through which we have lived. Scarely anything material or established which I was brought up to believe was permanent and vital, has lasted. Everything I was sure or taught to be sure was impossible, has happened."

At one point in the early 1930s, when Churchill's political fortunes were at their lowest ebb, his doubts deepened about whether he could still play a meaningful role under the conditions of the increasing scale of the world's problems. In his essay "A Second Choice" (which the political philosopher Harry Jaffa points out could be called "A Second *Chance*"), Churchill reflects on several of the controversial chapters in his life and wonders whether he would have chosen a different course of action. He wisely recognizes that, having "the same perplexities and hesitations, my same sense of proportion, my same guiding lights, my same onward thrust, my same limitations," he could not have altered his course without being an utterly different person.

But it is obvious that we never have as foreknowledge what we gain in hindsight. Churchill ended "A Second Choice" with a meditation that reads like an epitaph to his political career: "I do not seek to tread again the toilsome and dangerous path. Not even an opportunity of making a different set of mistakes and experiencing a different series of adventures and successes would lure me. How can I tell that the good fortune which has up to the present attended me with fair constancy would not be lacking at some critical moment in another chain of causation?"[3] What lay ahead, of course, was the greatest chapter of his long career, full of judgments and actions enough for an entire second lifetime. And in a sense, Churchill almost was reliving his past life: he began World War II in the same position—First Lord of the Admiralty—in which he began World War I. (In fact, when he returned to the admiralty office in 1939, he found the same maps, complete with the same pushpins, that he had left there in 1915.) He was facing the same foe, and that foe would be invading France very nearly along the same lines of advance as in World War I. Churchill was the only member of the war cabinet in 1939 who had been in the war cabinet in 1914, and his memories of the mistakes of the first war were prominent in his mind. This time the outcome would be different.

REAGAN CONFRONTED SIMILAR doubts in the American mind about the possibility of greatness and heroism. One of the corollaries of the 1970s-era idea of the "limits to growth" and diminished expectations was that heroism is anachronistic. Reagan went hard after this idea in his first moments in office. With his typical modesty, his answer was found within the democratic character of the nation itself. "We have every right to dream heroic dreams," Reagan said in his first inaugural address.

> Those who say that we are in a time when there are no heroes just don't know where to look. You can see heroes every day going in and out of factory

gates. Others, a handful in number, produce enough food to feed all of us and then the world beyond. You meet heroes across a counter, and they're on both sides of that counter. There are entrepreneurs with faith in themselves and faith in an idea who create new jobs, new wealth, and opportunity. They're individuals and families whose taxes support the government and whose voluntary gifts support church, charity, culture, art, and education. Their patriotism is quiet, but deep. Their values sustain our national life. Now, I have used the words "they" and "their" in speaking of these heroes. I could say "you" and "your," because I'm addressing the heroes of whom I speak—you, the citizens of this blessed land.

Reagan's 1981 inaugural was the first in the nation's history to be held on the west front of the Capitol building. From the west front, facing the Mall and looking out across the broad expanse of the nation, Reagan took note of the famous national monuments to "the giants upon whose shoulders we stand"—Washington, Jefferson, and above all Lincoln. About Lincoln, Reagan said, "Whoever in his heart would understand the meaning of America, will find it in the life of Abraham Lincoln." He also took note of the heroism of the Founders in establishing our constitutional order.

Then Reagan drew the nation's attention to another set of monuments visible in the far distance—the headstones of Arlington National Cemetery. Here Reagan made out the argument that self-government requires that all American citizens, in a sense, be heroes. "Each one of those markers is a monument to the kind of hero I spoke of earlier." He then selected the example of one ordinary American who did an extraordinary deed comparable in democratic merit to the giants such as Washington and Lincoln.

> Under one such marker lies a young man, Martin Treptow, who left his job in a small town barbershop in 1917 to go to France with the famed Rainbow Division. There, on the western front, he was killed trying to carry a message between battalions under heavy artillery fire. We're told that on his body was found a diary. On the flyleaf under the heading, "My Pledge," he had written these words: "America must win this war. Therefore I will work, I will save, I will sacrifice, I will endure, I will fight cheerfully and do my utmost, as if the issue of the whole struggle depended on me alone."

Reagan noted that current circumstances didn't require Americans to make the ultimate sacrifice as had Treptow; he drew an equivalence between the virtue of Treptow and ordinary citizens as a way of summoning Americans to think themselves worthy of their liberty. Reagan closed, "We can and will resolve the problems which now confront us. And, after all, why shouldn't we believe that? We are Americans."

That it required Ronald Reagan's fortitude and insight to remind Americans of their own innermost character at a moment of self-doubt raises the question of the paradox of greatness. Harry Jaffa observes, "The virtue of magnanimous men, we may say, becomes active primarily as a result of great crises, of situations of great need of their fellow-citizens."[4] Churchill faced the imminent destruction of his nation. Reagan in 1981, no less than Churchill in 1940, faced a crisis of the regime. The

American crisis of 1981 went beyond a loss of confidence to the question of whether the American presidency itself was still an adequate institution for modern conditions. In other words, there was doubt about whether constitutional government as practiced for 200 years in America could survive without major changes. After eight years of Reagan, intellectuals stopped asking these questions. (Indeed, his greatest achievement may be the one least mentioned—he proved that it was still possible to be an effective president.)

Would the greatness of either man be acknowledged without the extraordinary circumstances that called forth their action? Jaffa poses the question broadly: "What would William of Orange or Marlborough have been without Louis XIV, Pitt without Napoleon, Washington without George III, Lincoln without the slave interest, Churchill without Hitler?" William Manchester nearly suggests that Churchill *needed* Hitler: "Nothing, however, could match the satisfaction of directing his hostility outward, toward a great antagonist, a figure worthy of massive enmity. But as the years rolled by and he approached old age, the possibility of finding such an object became remote. . . . Then Churchill's prospects were dramatically altered. Adolf Hitler entered his life. By provoking his titanic wrath, the challenge from central Europe released enormous stores of long-suppressed vitality within him."[5] The final witness to this question is Hitler himself, who asked in a 1942 radio broadcast: "Churchill, what has he achieved in all his lifetime? . . . [H]ad this war not come, who would speak of Winston Churchill?"

Theologically inclined readers will recognize that this is a variation of the great question of whether God needed to create evil for good to exist, or whether God needs Satan in order to be God. Without resolving this large issue, we can see that its eternal nature points to a solution to the question of whether political greatness is still possible in modern times, and whether it requires extraordinary crises for someone to manifest greatness. To be sure, the spectacle of a great person matched up with his moment is how we come to recognize someone as a "statesman." Hitler was correct in a narrow sense: Without World War II Churchill would today be remembered as a colorful but semiobscure historical figure on par with F. E. Smith (Lord Birkenhead). Reagan's skills and insights were ideally matched to the circumstances of the 1980s. While he might have become president in another era, it is easy to envision counterfactual scenarios of an uneventful or unsuccessful presidency.

But even allowing for the role of chance and crisis as the necessary conditions for manifesting political greatness, the fact that it is easy to distinguish between Churchill and Hitler, between Reagan and the "evil empire," means that greatness is not purely circumstantial.[6] Greatness is ultimately a question of character. Good character does not change with the times: it has eternal qualities. Aristotle connects the honor that accrues to the magnanimous person with the virtues of friendship. This suggests that it is always within our grasp to cultivate the virtues of greatness as individuals, even if circumstances— crises—do not call forth the need for political greatness on the highest level. Churchill without World War II, and Reagan without the evil empire, are still admirable people in their own right, because they possessed the virtues that enabled them to act with greatness when the need arose. Both men would have been just as happy personally had those needs never arisen.

William Manchester employed as a hortatory theme the viewpoint that Churchill was "the last lion"—the last man of superlative virtue and courage, whose supreme greatness will never be seen again on the human stage. Manchester attributes Churchill's greatness precisely to the extent that Churchill was a Victorian anachronism in 1940, just as some of Reagan's own senior staff and public admirers see him as an American anachronism. Here we must suggest that for all of Manchester's fulsome admiration for Churchill and magnificence in describing his life, his premise is wrong. Roy Jenkins, Churchill's most recent biographer, says that explaining Churchill as a product of Victorian aristocracy is "unconvincing. . . . Churchill was far too many faceted, idiosyncratic and unpredictable a character to allow himself to be imprisoned by the circumstances of his birth."[7] John Lukacs adds, "Contrary to most accepted views we ought to consider that [Churchill] was not some kind of admirable remnant of a more heroic past. He was not The Last Lion. He was something else."[8] The "something else" at the root of Churchill's greatness in 1940 derived not from being a *Victorian* man but from being, in a larger sense, an *ancient* man—the kind of "great-souled man" contemplated in Aristotle and other classical authors.

The tides of history and the scale of modern life have not made obsolete or incommensurate the kind of large-souled greatness we associate with Churchill or Lincoln or George Washington. Of course all of us are powerfully affected by our environment and circumstances, yet the cases of Churchill and Reagan offer powerful refutation to the historicist premise that humans and human society are mostly corks bobbing on the waves of history. At the outset of this book we posed the question, Why were Churchill and Reagan virtually alone among their contemporaries in their particular insights and resolves? The answer must be that they transcended their environments and transformed their circumstances as only great men can do, and thereby bent history to their will. The political philosopher Leo Strauss wrote of Churchill, "A man like Churchill proves that the possibility of *megalophysis* [the great-souled man] exists today *exactly* as it did in the fifth century B.C."[9]

And so we have our answer to the question often voiced today: Can there be another Churchill, or another Reagan? The answer is plainly yes, though we must note that the greatness of statesmen is seldom recognized in their own time. Typically we only recognize greatness in hindsight. We should recall the severe criticism that Lincoln, Churchill, and Reagan all received while they were in office, and despite their loyal contemporary supporters, the suggestion that they would someday be honored as belonging among the ranks of the greatest statesmen would have excited a harrumph. There are sensible reasons for this. We lack foreknowledge of how events will be resolved. It was not evident that Churchill's and Reagan's designs would work out. Many critics expected disaster. The fundamental cause of contemporaneous doubt is the partisan division that is natural to political life at all times. Different ideological viewpoints reach radically different conclusions about present circumstances. One marker of great statesmen is that they are usually controversial during their time, and remain so in historical reckoning.

This brings us to the present, when another great world struggle is unfolding in front of us. Churchill's official biographer, Martin Gilbert, wrote recently:

> Although it can easily be argued that George W.
> Bush and Tony Blair face a far lesser challenge than
> Roosevelt and Churchill did—that the war on terror

is not a third world war—they may well, with the
passage of time and the opening of the archives,
join the ranks of Roosevelt and Churchill. Their
societies are too divided today to deliver a calm
judgment, and many of their achievements may be
in the future: when Iraq has a stable democracy,
with al-Qaeda neutralized, and when Israel and the
Palestinian Authority are independent democracies,
living side by side in constructive economic cooperation. . . . Any accurate assessment of Bush and
Blair must wait, perhaps a decade or longer, until
the record can be scrutinized.[10]

While we await the verdict of history on this prospect, it
is worth noting that in the immediate aftermath of September
11, the image and memory of Churchill were suddenly on
everyone's mind. President Bush keeps a bust of Churchill—a
gift from the British government—in the Oval Office. (Is the
comparison that far-fetched? In 1946 an American wrote to
Churchill about his Iron Curtain speech, "Just heard your
speech. You talk like a Texan, you act like a Texan, and God
bless you.") New York Mayor Rudy Giuliani was dubbed
"Churchill in a baseball cap," and *Time* magazine named
Giuliani its "Person of the Year" for 2001. In addition to recalling, by his visits to Ground Zero, scenes of Churchill visiting
bombed-out parts of London in 1940, Giuliani began reading
a Churchill biography when he got home at the end of a very
long day on September 11. *Time* magazine noted "a bright
magic at work when one great leader reaches into the past
and finds another waiting to guide him," prose which, historian John Ramsden points out, "effectively concedes that
[Time] had shortchanged Churchill in 1999, since it now

placed the highest value on all those qualities for which Churchill had stood but which had in 1999 seemed less valuable than others."[11]

One could suggest from *Time*'s reversal that Churchill might make a bid to be the man of the twenty-first century as well as the twentieth century. If so, this is because his example of the possibility of human greatness is not bound by time or circumstance. Leo Strauss took the death of Churchill in 1965 as the occasion to remind his students that "we have no higher duty, and no more pressing duty, than to remind ourselves and our students, of political greatness, of human greatness, of the peaks of human excellence. For we are supposed to train ourselves and others in seeing things as they are, and this means above all in seeing their greatness and their misery, their excellence and their vileness, their nobility and their triumphs, and therefore never to mistake mediocrity, however brilliant, for true greatness."

Contemplating the example of Churchill and his influence on Reagan gives us confidence that even though the mountaintops may be often shrouded in fog, we can still tell the difference between peaks and valleys.

NOTES

CHAPTER I. WHAT IS GREATNESS?

1. Although quoting Churchill is a bipartisan enthusiasm, historian John Ramsden noted that "Bill Clinton made few rhetorical gestures towards Churchill in an eight-year presidency of the United States, being perhaps the first President since Herbert Hoover to neglect that duty." John Ramsden, *Man of the Century: Winston Churchill and His Legend Since 1945* (New York: Columbia University Press, 2002), p. 579.
2. The original Churchill remark Reagan paraphrased was: "I have not become the King's First Minister in order to preside over the liguidation of the British Empire."
3. Aristotle, *Nicomachean Ethics,* Book VI.
4. Aristotle, *Nicomachean Ethics,* Book VI, 1143a. "Practical wisdom issues commands," Aristotle writes. "Its end is to tell us what we ought to do and what we ought not to do. Understanding, on the other hand, only passes judgment."
5. Quoted in Gertrude Himmelfarb, "The Roar," *The New Republic,* November 26, 2001, p. 26.

CHAPTER 2. PARALLEL LIVES I

1. Churchill's intellectual qualities were not universally recognized during his lifetime. Margot Asquith wrote in her diary at the time of Churchill's fortieth birthday, "What is it that gives Winston his pre-eminence? It is certainly not his mind. I have said long ago and with truth Winston has a very noisy mind. Certainly not his judgment—he is constantly very wrong indeed. . . . *It is of course his courage and color—his amazing mixture of industry and enterprise* [emphasis added]."

2. Robert Rhodes James, *Churchill: Four Faces and the Man* (London: Penguin, 1969), p. 57.

3. Winston Churchill, *My Early Life: 1874–1904* (New York: Charles Scribner's Sons, 1930), p. 59; President Reagan, remarks, January 27, 1984.

4. Churchill worked on a screenplay of the life of King George V at the request of Hollywood producer Alexander Korda in 1934. Korda paid Churchill 10,000 pounds for the work. Although Churchill completed the script, the film was never made. The editor for Reagan's postpresidential memoirs, *An American Life,* published in 1990 by Simon & Schuster, was Michael Korda, who is Alexander Korda's nephew. Ronald Reagan, *An American Life: The Autobiography* (New York: Simon & Schuster, 1990).

5. Fortunately for Churchill and for history, the industrialist Henry Strakosch assumed Churchill's debts.

6. Reagan wrote to Laurence Beilenson in a personal letter in 1986, "You know, those people who thought being an actor was no proper training for this job were way off base. Every day I find myself thankful for those long days at the negotiating table with Harry Cohen, Freeman, the broth-

ers Warner et al." Kiron K. Skinner, Annelise Anderson, and Martin Anderson, eds., *Reagan: A Life in Letters* (New York: Free Press, 2003), p. 428.

7. Secret Session speech to the House of Commons, June 20, 1940.

8. William Manchester, *The Last Lion: Winston Spencer Churchill, Alone, 1932–1940* (Boston: Little Brown, 1988), p. 34.

9. Kiron K. Skinner, Annelise Anderson, and Martin Anderson, eds., *Reagan in His Own Hand: The Writings of Ronald Reagan That Reveal His Revolutionary Vision for America* (New York: Free Press, 2001), p. xx.

10. See *Reagan in His Own Hand, The Writings of Ronald Reagan That Reveal His Revolutionary Vision for America, Reagan: A Life in Letters,* and *Reagan's Path to Victory* (all edited by Skinner, Anderson, and Anderson, published by Free Press.)

11. D. J. Wenden, "Churchill, Radio, and Cinema," in Robert Blake and William Roger Louis, eds., *Churchill: A Major New Assessment of His Life in Peace and War* (New York: Norton, 1993), p. 223.

12. Quoted in William Manchester, *Winston Spencer Churchill: The Last Lion,* vol. 1: *Visions of Glory 1874–1932* (Boston: Little Brown, 1983), p. 802.

13. James, in *Churchill: Four Faces and the Man,* p. 108.

14. See Richard J. Powell and Dan Schloyer, "Public Presidential Appeals and Congressional Floor Votes," *Congress and the Presidency,* Autumn 2003.

15. *The Nation,* April 11, 1981, p. 420.

16. Lou Cannon, *President Reagan: The Role of a Lifetime* (New York: Simon & Schuster, 1991), p. 338.

17. Quoted in Martin Gilbert, "In Search of Churchill's Character," in Harry Jaffa, ed., *Statesmanship: Essays in*

Honor of Winston Churchill (Durham: Carolina Academic Press, 1981), p. 21.

18. Cannon, *President Reagan: Role of a Lifetime,* p. 125.

19. Kay Halle, compiler, *The Irrepressible Churchill: Through His Own Words and the Eyes of His Contemporaries* (London: Robson Books, 1985), p. 172.

20. PBS TV's Paul Duke—to pick just one example—expressed the general consensus of the Washington media when he wrote in 1986 that Reagan is "intellectually lazy, inattentive to details and sometimes ignorant of important developments." Paul Duke, ed., *Beyond Reagan: The Politics of Upheaval* (New York: Warner Books, 1986).

21. Anthony Storr, "The Man," in James, ed., *Churchill: Four Faces and the Man,* pp. 225–26.

22. Cannon, *President Reagan: Role of a Lifetime,* p. 231.

23. Garry Wills, *Reagan's America* (New York: Doubleday, 1986), p. 475.

24. Isaiah Berlin, "Winston Churchill in 1940," *Personal Impressions* (London: The Hogarth Press, 1981), p. 9.

25. Winston S. Churchill, *Savrola: A Novel* (Random House edition, 1956; originally published 1900), p. 34.

26. Remarks to students at Fallston High School, Fallston, Maryland, December 4, 1985.

27. Cannon, *President Reagan: Role of a Lifetime,* p. 61.

28. Cannon, *President Reagan: Role of a Lifetime,* p. 55.

29. Cited in Eliot A. Cohen, *Supreme Command: Soldiers, Statesmen, and Leadership in Time of War* (New York: Free Press, 2002), p. 98.

30. Cannon, *President Reagan: Role of a Lifetime,* p. 172.

31. Haynes Johnson, *Sleepwalking Through History: America in the Reagan Years* (New York: Norton, 1991), p. 41.

32. Cannon, *President Reagan: Role of a Lifetime,* p. 36.

33. WSC to Clem, April 27, 1908. Mary Soames, ed., *Winston and Clementine: The Personal Letters of the Churchills* (Boston: Houghton Mifflin, 2001), p. 9.

34. Nancy Reagan, *I Love You, Ronnie: The Letters of Ronald Reagan to Nancy Reagan* (New York: Random House, 2000), p. 11.

35. Storr, "The Man," p. 205.

36. Cannon, *President Reagan: Role of a Lifetime*, p. 33.

37. Duke, *Beyond Reagan*, p. 134, 136.

38. Plumb in James, *Churchill: Four Faces and the Man*, p. 126.

39. Halle, *Irrepresible Churchill*, p. 177.

40. During the 1980 campaign Reagan told Charlie Rose on PBS TV, "Show me an executive who works long, overtime hours, and I'll show you a bad executive." (Quoted in Cannon, *President Reagan: Role of a Lifetime* p. 125.)

41. Winston S. Churchill, *Great Contemporaries* (New York: Norton, 1991; originally published in London by Thornton Butterworth in 1937), p. 140.

42. Martin Gilbert, *Winston S. Churchill* (London: Heinemann, 1976), p. 995.

43. Violet Bonham Carter, *Winston Churchill: An Intimate Portrait* (New York: Harcourt, Brace & World, 1965), p. 4.

44. Richard M. Langworth, "Ronald Reagan, 1911–2004), *Finest Hour*, No. 123 (Summer 2004), p. 17.

45. Manchester, *The Last Lion*, vol. 1, p. 768.

46. By contrast, it was typical of Jimmy Carter to use the personal pronoun "I" between 50 and 100 times in speeches boasting of his record as governor of Georgia.

47. Nancy Reagan, *I Love You, Ronnie*, p. 11.

48. Reagan's immediate sequel in the Westminster speech makes clear he viewed this problem as a continuum: "Now I am aware that among us here and throughout Europe

there is legitimate disagreement over the extent to which the public sector should play a role in a nation's economy and life. But on one point all of us are united: our abhorrence of dictatorship in all its forms."

49. Harry V. Jaffa, "Can There Be Another Winston Churchill?," in Jaffa, ed., *Statesmanship*, p. 38.

50. Churchill's postwar opponent Clement Attlee probably offered the most probative description of Churchill, comparing him to a layer cake: "One layer is certainly seventeenth century. The eighteenth in him is obvious! There was the nineteenth century and a large slice, of course, of the twentieth century; and another curious layer which may possibly have been the twenty-first." (Cited in Halle, *Irrepressible Churchill,* p. 217.)

CHAPTER 3. PARALLEL LIVES II

1. Ronald Reagan, *An American Life: The Autobiography* (New York: Simon & Schuster, 1990), p. 28.

2. I owe this piece of trivia to the inexhaustible researches of Michael Barone, who prowled through old property records in each of Reagan's boyhood hometowns.

3. Among other parallels, both men record among their earliest childhood memories the cases of drowning in nearby bodies of water.

4. Anthony Storr, "The Man," in Robert Rhodes James, *Churchill: Four Faces and the Man* (London: Penguin, 1969), p. 250.

5. Reagan, *An American Life*, p. 24.

6. Winston Churchill, *My Early Life: 1874–1904* (New York: Charles Scribner's Sons, 1930), p. 19.

7. Ronald Reagan, with Richard G. Hubler, *Where's the Rest of Me?: The Autobiography of Ronald Reagan* (New York: Karz, 1981; reprint of the 1965 edition), p. 9.

8. Churchill, *My Early Life*, p. 46.

9. Churchill, *My Early Life*, pp. 4–5.

10. Reagan, *Where's the Rest of Me?*, p. 3.

11. Mary Soames, ed., *Winston and Clementine: The Personal Letters of the Churchills* (New York: Houghton Mifflin, 2001), pp. xv–xvi.

12. Quoted in Soames, *Winston and Clementine*, p. 17.

13. Randolph S. Churchill, *Winston S. Churchill: Young Statesman, 1901–1914* (Boston: Houghton Mifflin, 1967), p. 266.

14. CSC to WSC, April 27, 1909, in Soames, *Winston and Clementine*, p. 21.

15. WSC to CSC, August 9, 1929, in Soames, *Winston and Clementine*, p. 336.

16. Noemie Emery, "First Dad: The Burden of Having a President as Father," *The Weekly Standard*, June 16, 2003, p. 30.

CHAPTER 4. THE EDUCATION OF STATESMEN

1. Neither did Aristotle: See *Nicomachean Ethics*, Book VI, 1140b, 20–25.

2. Winston Churchill, *My Early Life: 1874–1904* (New York: Charles Scribner's Sons, 1930), pp. 38–39.

3. Churchill, *My Early Life*, p. 42.

4. Garry Wills, *Reagan's America* (New York: Doubleday, 1986), p. 58.

5. Ronald Reagan, with Richard G. Hubler, *Where's the Rest of Me?: The Autobiography of Ronald Reagan* (New York: Karz, 1981; reprint of the 1965 edition), pp. 28–29.

6. Edmund Morris, *Dutch: A Memoir of Ronald Reagan* (New York: Random House, 1999), p. 71.

7. Churchill records his disappointment with the hollow league in terms that suggest he understands what humbug this cause really was: "The Entertainments Protection League might have made real progress. It might, in those early nineties, when so many things were in the making, have marshaled a public opinion so vigilant throughout the English-speaking world, and pronounced a warning so impressive, that the mighty United States themselves might have been saved from Prohibition! Here again we see the footprints of Fate, but they turned off the pleasant lawns on to a dry and stony highway."

8. Churchill, *My Early Life*, p. 57.

9. Churchill, *My Early Life*, p. 109.

10. Churchill's self-education has its critics. John Charmley wrote that "it was self-education with a limited purpose; it provided no training in learning how to think, how to weigh arguments, and how to judge your own ideas against those of others." From *Churchill, The End of Glory: A Political Biography* (New York: Harcourt, Brace, 1993), p. 16.

11. Kenneth W. Thompson, *Winston Churchill's Worldview: Statesmanship and Power* (Baton Rouge: Louisiana State University Press, 1983), p. 116.

12. Jules Witcover and Richard Cohen, "Where's the Rest of Ronald Reagan?," *Esquire*, March 1976, p. 92.

13. Reagan's fear of flying offers a sharp contrast to Churchill, who couldn't be kept out of airplanes. Churchill learned to fly back when planes still had open cockpits, and had to be forcibly persuaded by his family and friends to quit flying at a time when the risks were very high.

14. This occurred in 1987. In 1984 Reagan did respond to a request for his current reading from the *Baltimore Sun*, and provided the following five titles: William Rusher, *The*

Rise of the Right; David Lamb, *The Africans;* Frank van der Linden, *The Turning Point: Jefferson's Battle for the Presidency;* Sir John Hackett, *The Third World War;* Richard Shultz and Roy Godson, *Dezinformatsia.* Also, at the time of his first summit meeting with Mikhail Gorbachev in Geneva in 1985, Reagan read Suzanne Massie's *Land of the Firebird,* a cultural history of Russia.

15. Speech at the University of Miami, February 26, 1946.

16. John Colville, *The Fringes of Power: 10 Downing Street Diaries, 1939–1955* (New York: Norton, 1985), p. 125.

CHAPTER 5. FAITH AND DESTINY

1. William Manchester, *Winston Spencer Churchill: The Last Lion* vol. 1, *Visions of Glory, 1874–1932* (Boston: Little, Brown, 1983), p. 177.

2. John Colville, *The Fringes of Power,* p. 128.

3. Kiron K. Skinner, Annelise Anderson, and Martin Anderson, eds., *Reagan: A Life in Letters* (New York: Free Press, 2003), p. 276.

4. Reagan to Mrs. Van Voohis, in Skinner, Anderson, and Anderson, eds., *Reagan: A Life in Letters,* pp. 277–78. In 1984 Reagan wrote to Sister Mary Ignatius, "Abe Lincoln once said that he would be the most stupid human on this footstool called Earth if he thought for one minute he could fulfill the obligations of the office he held without help from one who was wiser and stronger than all others. I understand what he meant completely."

5. Quoted in Paul Kengor, *God and Ronald Reagan* (New York: Regan Books, 2004), p. iii. For additional insight into Reagan's spiritual life, see also Mary Beth Brown, *Hand of Providence: The Strong and Quiet Faith of Ronald Reagan* (Nashville: WND Books, 2004).

6. WSC speech, January 1, 1920, cited in Martin Gilbert, *Churchill's Political Philosophy* (New York: Oxford University Press, 1982), p. 77.

7. Winston Churchill, *My Early Life: 1874–1904* (New York: Charles Scribner's Sons, 1930), p. 115.

8. Churchill, *My Early Life,* p. 117.

9. "We reject, however, with scorn all those learned and laboured myths that Moses was but a legendary figure upon whom the priesthood and the people hung their essential social, moral and religious ordinances. We believe that the most scientific view, the most up-to-date and rationalistic conception, will find its fullest satisfaction in taking the Bible story literally, and in identifying one of the greatest of human beings with the most decisive leap forward ever discernable in the human story. . . . We may be sure that all these things happened just as they are set out according to Holy Writ." From "Moses: The Leader of a People," in Winston Churchill, *Thoughts and Adventures* (London: Thornton Butterworth, 1932), p. 293. Reagan expressed the same scorn for modernist biblical criticism, writing in a 1978 radio address: "It was disturbing therefore to read that in many Christian seminaries there is an increasing tendency to minimize [Christ's] divinity, to reject the miracle of his birth and regard him as merely human."

10. I owe this observation to my great teacher Harry Jaffa, who noted this aspect of Churchill's outlook in an essay entitled "Can There Be Another Winston Churchill?," in Harry Jaffa, ed., *Statesmanship: Essays in Honor of Winston Churchill* (Durham: Carolina Academic Press, 1981), p. 29.

11. Though this is often claimed in Churchill biographies, the British staged cavalry charges in the Boer War two years later.

12. Churchill, *My Early Life*, p. 276.
13. Churchill, "With the Grenadiers," in Winston Churchill, *Thoughts and Adventures* (London: Thornton Butterworth, 1932), p. 71.
14. Reagan to Jean B. Wright, March 13, 1984, in Skinner, Anderson, and Anderson, eds., *Reagan: A Life in Letters*, p. 6.

CHAPTER 6. THE PATH
TO CONSERVATISM

1. John Colville, in John Wheeler-Bennett, ed., *Action This Day: Working with Churchill* (London: Macmillan, 1968), pp. 48–49.
2. Jack Nelson, "The Reagan Legacy," in Paul Duke, ed., *Beyond Reagan: The Politics of Upheaval* (New York: Warner Books, 1986), p. 110.
3. Alan Wolfe, "What Is to Be Done?" *The Nation*, November 22, 1980, p. 534.
4. Curtis Gans: "A Crosscurrent, Not a Watershed," *The Nation*, December 13, 1980, p. 632.
5. Derek Leebaert, *The Fifty-Year Wound: The True Price of America's Cold War Victory* (Boston: Little, Brown, 2002), p. 589.
6. Churchill's fondness for the Democratic Party in America stems in part from the fact his first contact with American politics was through Bourke Cochran, a free-trade, laissez-faire Democrat.
7. In his 1980 nomination-acceptance speech, Reagan said, "The time is now to redeem promises once made to the American people by another candidate, in another time and another place. He said, '. . . For three long years I have been going up and down this country preaching that government—federal, state, and local—costs too much. I shall

not stop that preaching. As an immediate program of action, we must abolish useless offices. We must eliminate unnecessary functions of government. . . . I propose to you, my friends, and through you that government of all kinds, big and little, be made solvent and that the example be set by the President of the United States and his cabinet.' So said Franklin Delano Roosevelt in is acceptance speech to the Democratic National Convention in July 1932." Reagan's use of FDR drove liberals out of their mind. Arkansas's young governor, Bill Clinton, complained, "Everyone can quote him, but his words out of context mean nothing."

8. For a fresh and thorough review of the subtleties of the New Deal, see Robert Eden, ed., *The New Deal and Its Legacy: Critique and Reappraisal* (Westport, CT: Greenwood Press, 1989).

9. The distinction between these two kinds of liberalism is the subject of the first five chapters of my book *The Age of Reagan: The Fall of the Old Liberal Order, 1964–1980* (Roseville, CA: Prima, 2001).

10. Winston Churchill, *Thoughts and Adventures* (London: Thornton Butterworth, 1932), pp. 255–56.

11. See his essay "Parliamentary Government and the Economic Problem," in *Thoughts and Adventures,* pp. 229–41.

12. "Looking Out a Window," in Kiron K. Skinner, Annelise Anderson, and Martin Anderson, eds., *Reagan in His Own Hand* (New York: Free Press, 2001), p. 18.

13. Churchill, *Thoughts and Adventures,* p. 39.

14. Speech at Kinnaird Hall, May 8, 1908, in Robert Rhodes James, ed., *Winston S. Churchill: His Complete Speeches,* vol. 1 (London: Chelsea House, 1974), p. 1028. Churchill went on to dissect socialist politics with great acuity: "I

think the exalted idea of the Socialists—a universal brotherhood, owning all things in common—is not always supported by the evidence of their practice. They put before us a creed of universal self-sacrifice. They preach it in the language of spite and envy, or hatred, and all uncharitableness. They tell us that we should dwell together in unity and comradeship. They are themselves split into twenty obscure factions, who hate and abuse each other more than they hate and abuse us."

15. Robert Rhodes James, *Churchill: A Study in Failure, 1900–1939* (New York: World Publishing, 1970), p. 36.

16. Lou Cannon, *President Reagan: Role of a Lifetime* (New York: Simon & Schuster, 1991), p. 43.

17. Cited in Martin Gilbert, *Winston S. Churchill: Road to Victory, 1941–1945* (Boston: Houghton Mifflin, 1986), p. 1252.

18. Speech to the American Conservative Union, February 6, 1977.

19. Churchill's more whimsical reflection was "Never stand so high upon a principle that you cannot lower it to suit the circumstances."

20. Speech to the American Conservative Union, February 6, 1977.

21. In 1983 Reagan said to a group of congressmen visiting the White House that he had not realized that most of the Soviets' nuclear arsenal consisted of land-based missiles, which is why the Soviets considered unfair Reagan's proposal to cut land-based missiles by half. The visiting congressmen were appalled at Reagan's seeming ignorance, and the story soon found its way to the news media. There's only one problem with this story: it isn't true that Reagan didn't know the Soviets' nuclear force structure.

Reagan's own handwritten notes and articles from before he became president show that he had detailed knowledge about the Soviets' force structure and how it compared with the U.S. force structure, right down to the number of warheads carried on U.S. and Soviet ICBMs. This peculiar example of Reagan suppressing his own knowledge is reviewed and discussed by Tim H. Blessing and Anne A. Skleder, "Top Down: A General Overview of Present Research on Ronald Reagan's Doctrinal Presidency," in Richard S. Conley, ed., *Reassessing the Reagan Presidency* (Lanham, MD: University Press of America, 2003), pp. 8–10. Blessing and Skleder write that "in instance after instance, Reagan hid the nature and depth of his knowledge."

CHAPTER 7. CHURCHILL AND REAGAN ON DOMESTIC POLICY

1. Transcript, "The Advocates," PBS Television, December 1, 1970, p. 11.
2. William Manchester, *The Last Lion: Winston Spencer Churchill*, vol. 1: *Visions of Glory* (Boston: Little, Brown, 1983), vol. 1, p. 22.
3. Remarks to the New York City Partnership, January 14, 1982.
4. Mansion House speech, June 11, 1925.
5. See especially his radio broadcast on "Employment" from July 1978, in Kiron K. Skinner, Annelise Anderson, and Martin Anderson, eds., *Reagan's Path to Victory: The Shaping of Ronald Reagan's Vision: Selected Writings* (New York: Free Press, 2004), pp. 343–44, and "Unemployment," radio address of August 15, 1977, in *Reagan in His Own Hand: The Writings of Ronald Reagan That Reveal His*

Revolutionary Vision for America (New York: The Free Press, 2001), pp. 267–68.

6. Budget Address, House of Commons, April 15, 1929.

7. Cited in Paul Addison, *Churchill on the Home Front* (London: Pimlico, 1992), p. 282.

8. "Humphrey-Hawkins Bill," radio broadcast, September 21, 1976, in Skinner, Anderson, and Anderson, eds., *Reagan's Path to Victory,* p. 72.

9. Robert Kaiser, "Those Old Reaganisms May Be Brought Back to Haunt Him," *Washington Post,* September 2, 1980, p. A2.

10. As Reagan explained in his 1976 radio address, "The annual plan would involve government allocating resources including labor. It creates national government machinery for planning virtually every aspect of American life, projecting national goals for production, purchasing power, etc." This was an accurate description of the aims of Humphrey-Hawkins, which Democratic investment banker Felix Rohatyn described as "the first step toward state planning of the economy."

11. F. A. Hayek, *The Road to Serfdom* (Chicago: University of Chicago Press, 1944), p. 184.

12. Election address, June 4, 1945.

13. The complete line was "Extremism in defense of liberty is no vice; moderation in the defense of justice is no virtue."

14. Cited in Addison, *Churchill on the Home Front,* p. 383.

15. Speech to the London Chambers of Commerce Association, March 18, 1908.

16. *Time,* November 19, 1945, p. 29.

17. Kiron K. Skinner, Annelise Anderson, and Martin Anderson, eds., *Reagan: A Life in Letters* (New York: The Free Press, 2003), p. 273.

18. Readers interested in learning more about supply-side economics should see any of the fine narrative and analytical books covering the idea and Reagan's experience, such as Paul Craig Roberts, *The Supply-Side Revolution* (Cambridge, MA: Harvard University Press, 1984); William A. Niskanen, *Reaganomics* (New York: Oxford University Press, 1988); Robert Bartley, *The Seven Fat Years* (New York: Free Press, 1992); Lawrence B. Lindsay, *The Growth Experiment: How the New Tax Policy is Transforming the U.S. Economy* (New York: Basic Books, 1990). Martin Feldstein, ed., *American Economic Policy in the 1980s* (Chicago: University of Chicago Press, 1994); John W. Sloan, *The Reagan Effect: Economics and Presidential Leadership* (Lawrence: University Press of Kansas, 1999); Martin Anderson, *Revolution: The Reagan Legacy* (New York: Harcourt, Brace, 1988), Michael J. Boskin, *Reagan and the Economy: The Successes, Failures, and Unfinished Agenda* (San Francisco: Institute for Contemporary Studies, 1987); Richard B. McKenzie, *What Went Right in the 1980s* (San Francisco: Pacific Research Institute, 1994).

19. Budget address, House of Commons, April 28, 1925.

20. Budget address, House of Commons, May 25, 1925.

21. Budget address, House of Commons, June 15, 1925.

22. Cited in Peter Clarke, "Churchill's Economic Ideas," in Robert Blake and Roger Louis, eds., *Churchill: A Major New Assessment of His Life in Peace and War* (New York: Norton, 1993), p. 89.

23. Reagan, question-and-answer session with state and local government officials, May 28, 1981.

24. See Henry Pelling, "Churchill and the Labour Movement," in Blake and Louis, eds., *Churchill: A Major New Assessment*, pp. 113–28.

25. Another Reagan parallel: Reagan noted the mismatch between pockets of unemployment and pockets of jobs going begging, and asked in a 1975 radio address, "Why not a periodic census of job skills, which are in surplus, which are in short supply and where?"

26. Quoted in Addison, *Churchill on the Home Front,* p. 146.

27. Norman Rose, *Churchill: The Unruly Giant* (New York: Free Press, 1994), p. 95.

28. Manchester, *The Last Lion,* vol. 1, p. 804.

29. "I have always supported the union shop," Reagan said in his first inaugural address as governor of California in 1967, "even though that includes a certain amount of compulsion with regard to union membership."

30. This, despite a series of anti-Reagan TV commercials that the public employees union (AFSCME) began running in thirteen major markets.

31. After installing Remirro de Orca, "a cruel and ready man," to govern the previously unruly province of Romagna, Borgia recognized that de Orca had become hated by the people and had outlived his usefulness. So Borgia had him cut in two pieces, and left his body in the piazza at Cesena, with a piece of wood and a bloody knife beside him.

CHAPTER 8. FROM FULTON TO BERLIN

1. This vignette is recorded by Dinesh D'Souza in *Ronald Reagan: How an Ordinary Man Became an Extraordinary Leader* (New York: The Free Press, 1998), p. 1.

2. William Manchester commented on this phrase: "If this rhetoric sounds extravagant, it should be remembered that the Bolshevik holocaust—five years of fighting, pestilence, and famine—cost fifteen million lives."

3. Martin Gilbert, *Winston S. Churchill,* vol. 4 (London: Heinemann, 1975), p. 430.

4. Winston S. Churchill, *The World Crisis: The Aftermath* (London: Thornton Butterworth, 1929), pp. 73, 74, 459.

5. Winston S. Churchill, "Mass Effects in Modern Life," in Winston Churchill, *Thoughts and Adventures* (London: Thornton Butterworth, 1932), p. 259.

6. For a more complete treatment of this subject, see Chapter 9, "Détente and Its Discontents," in Steven F. Hayward, *The Age of Reagan: The Fall of the Old Liberal Order, 1964–1980* (Roseville, CA: Prima, 2001).

7. John Colville, *The Fringes of Power: 10 Downing Street Diaries, 1939–1955* (New York: W.W. Norton, 1985), p. 658. This was said six weeks before Stalin died. Stalin died. Colville died in 1987, at the age of seventy-two, shortly before the final collapse of the Soviet Union began. Churchill also referred to the possibility of Communist collapse in a 1949 speech at the Massachusetts Institute of Technology: "Laws just or unjust may govern men's actions. Tyrannies may restrain and regulate their words. The machinery of propaganda may pack their minds with falsehoods and deny them truth for many generations of time. But the soul of man this held in trance, or frozen in a long night, can be awakened by a spark coming from God knows where, and in a moment the whole structure of lies and oppression is on trial for its life. Peoples in bondage need never despair."

8. Churchill contemplated at the end of World War II the division of Europe that would necessarily come with Soviet occupation of the East. He remarked to Charles de Gaulle that while the Soviets were a hungry wolf now, "after the meal comes the digestion period." The Soviet Union,

Churchill thought, would not be able to digest the peoples of Eastern Europe. John Lukacs relates and reflects upon this story in several of his books. See, e.g., *1945 Year Zero: The Shaping of the Modern Age* (New York: Doubleday, 1978), p. 60.

9. At other times Reagan characterized Communism as "another sad, bizarre chapter in human history whose last pages even now are being written."

10. Paul Kengor offers a copious roundup of these admissions in Chapter 16 of is book *God and Ronald Reagan: A Spiritual Life* (New York: Regan Books, 2004).

11. Strobe Talbott, *The Russians and Reagan* (New York: Vintage, 1984), p. 33. Talbott continued, "After all, the Soviets do lie, cheat, and reserve the right to commit any crime; they do preside over the last great empire on earth; and many aspects of their behavior, both toward their own people and toward those of other lands, are so offensive and threatening to the democratic and human values that evil is not an outrageous characterization of them."

12. Reagan was not alone in this perception. In 1977 Norman Podhoretz wrote, "I have been struck very forcibly by certain resemblances between the United States today and Great Britain in the years after the first world war. . . . The parallels with England in 1937 are here, and this revival of the culture of appeasement ought to be troubling our sleep." Now SALT II seemed to confirm the worst fears of conservatives about American appeasement, and the argument over SALT II and the military balance between the United States and the Soviets was very nearly identical, in form and substance, to Churchill's argument about the airpower balance between Britain and Nazi Germany in the late 1930s. Senator Henry Jackson complained, "To

enter a treaty which favors the Soviets as this one does on the ground that we will be in a worse position without it, is appeasement in its purest form. . . . It is all ominously reminiscent of Great Britain in the 1930s." Eugene Rostow went even further, noting that the arguments made in favor of SALT II were identical to the arguments made on behalf of the Washington Naval Treaty of 1922, which not only failed to prevent World War II but arguably helped to bring it on.

13. *National Review,* March 16, 1979, p. 334. Ironically, Carter was highly conscious of the potential comparison. According to Carter's chief of staff Hamilton Jordan, Carter refused to use an umbrella in the rain in Vienna after meeting Soviet leader Leonid Brezhnev and signing an arms control treaty for fear it would summon images of Neville Chamberlain's appeasement. The irony of this circumstance is that Carter read Churchill's *The Gathering Storm* around the time of the Soviet invasion of Afghanistan, and remarked to *Time* magazine's Hugh Sidey, "Nobody sent a clear signal to Hitler. War became inevitable. We are not going to let that happen."

14. Richard Allen memo to Governor Reagan, August 25, 1978, Deaver-Hannaford Papers, Box 3, Ronald Reagan Presidential Library.

15. Iklé letter to Hannaford, March 8, 1979, Deaver-Hannaford Papers, Box 2, Ronald Reagan Presidential Library.

16. Remarks at White House ceremony, November 11, 1982. This was the day after the death of Leonid Brezhnev.

17. Remarks to Jewish Holocaust survivors, April 11, 1983.

18. Klaus Larres, *Churchill's Cold War: The Politics of Personal Diplomacy* (New Haven: Yale University Press, 2002), p. xv.

19. John Lukacs, "Blood, Sweat, and Fears," *The New Republic*, January 13, 2003, p. 37.

20. John Lukacs, *Churchill: Visionary, Statesman, Historian* (New Haven: Yale University Press, 2002), p. 26.

21. I owe this observation, and much else besides, to John Lukacs, in his several books discussing Churchill's statecraft.

22. Oval Office interview with print reporters, December 23, 1981.

23. Remarks at campaign rally, Grand Forks, North Dakota, October 17, 1986.

24. Hedrick Smith, "The Right Against Reagan," *New York Times Magazine*, January 17, 1988, p. 38.

25. George Will, 1989, in D'Souza, *Ronald Reagan*, p. 185.

26. David Binder, "Revival of the Berlin Wall Debate: If We Had Knocked It Down . . . ," *New York Times*, August 14, 1986, p. A-16.

27. Gorbachev wrote in the *New York Times* the week of Reagan's funeral, "I don't know whether we would have been able to agree and to insist on the implementation of our agreements with a different person at the helm of American government. . . . [Reagan] was not dogmatic; he was looking for negotiations and cooperation." (*New York Times*, June 7, 2004.)

CHAPTER 9. MEASURING GREAT STATESMEN

1. *Time* chose Albert Einstein as its "Person of the Century" instead. John Ramsden observed that Einstein would probably have disagreed: "Einstein had himself argued that bad politics were more likely to bring the world to

grief than bad science, and hence had implicitly endorsed Churchill's claim over his own."

2. A British Department of Education video on World War II in 1995 included just 14 seconds about Churchill out of a total program of 35 minutes.

3. Winston Churchill, *Thoughts and Adventures* (London: Thornton Butterworth, 1932), p. 19.

4. Harry V. Jaffa, *Thomism and Aristotelianism* (Westport, CT: Greenwood Press, 1979; originally published University of Chicago Press, 1952), p. 128.

5. William Manchester, *The Last Lion, Winston Spencer Churchill*, vol. 1: *Visions of Glory, 1874–1932* (Boston: Little, Brown, 1983), pp. 24–25.

6. As Leo Strauss put it, "The contrast between the indomitable and magnanimous statesman and the insane tyrant—this spectacle in its clear simplicity was one of the great lessons which men can learn, at any time."

7. Roy Jenkins, *Churchill: A Biography* (New York: Farrar, Straus and Giroux, 2001), p. 3.

8. John Lukacs, *Churchill: Visionary, Statesman, Historian* (New Haven: Yale University Press, 2002), p. 17.

9. Leo Strauss, letter to Karl Lowith, August 20, 1946, reprinted in the *Independent Journal of Philosophy*, vol. 4 (1983), p. 111.

10. Martin Gilbert, "Statesmen for These Times," *The Observer*, December 26, 2004.

11. John Ramsden, *Man of the Century: Churchill and His Legend Since 1945* (New York: Columbia University Press, 2002), pp. 586–87.

ACKNOWLEDGMENTS

READERS HAVE been asking me since the fall of 2001 when they can expect the sequel to the first volume of my history of Ronald Reagan and his place in American political life, *The Age of Reagan: The Fall of the Old Liberal Order, 1964–1980*. I have been working on the second volume, tentatively titled *The Age of Reagan: Lion at the Gate, 1980–1989*, for three years. While I was working on the second volume, an unexpected discovery led to the origin of this short book and a brief interruption of the larger project.

In writing *The Age of Reagan: Lion at the Gate*, I thought it worth four or five paragraphs to explore Reagan's frequent use of Churchill (he quoted Churchill three times as often as any other president) and what that told us about his style of leadership. Five thousand words later I was still going, having discovered while working through the material that the extensive parallels between Reagan and Churchill were profound and important. I became especially interested in what those parallels tell us about political genius and the makings of great statesmen.

I had no larger thoughts about what to do with this

193

comparison until I visited the Hoover Institution at Stanford University in 2004 as a national fellow. I decided to try out the Reagan-Churchill comparison in a seminar with a number of the Reaganites in residence at Hoover. Longtime Reagan adviser Martin Anderson suggested that a comparison of Reagan and Churchill was worthy of a full book-length treatment. Marty's suggestion germinated quickly into this book, and I am grateful to him for inspiring me to pursue this project. I also thank him and his wife, Annelise, for their extensive work in unearthing and publishing Reagan's handwritten letters, speeches, and radio addresses, which have been instrumental in revealing an unknown side of our fortieth president.

A number of other people deserve thanks and recognition for their help and inspiration for my work on both Churchill and Reagan: Larry Arnn, Mark Burson, Martin Gilbert, Kirby Hanson, John Lukacs, Ed Meese, Paul Rahe, Peter Robinson, Peter Schramm, and Spencer Warren have provided invaluable help and inspiration. Lou Cannon, the dean of Reagan reporters and biographers, has provided essential insights and encouragement. I owe much to Professor James Muller of the University of Alaska, who has done intensive original work on Churchill's education. I could not have written Chapters 3 and 4 without his example. I could not have written this at all had I not learned at the feet of Harry Jaffa. Finally, no one should work on Churchill without making use of the Churchill Centre in Washington, D.C., and especially two key figures behind that enterprise, Dan Myers and Richard Langworth. Bookmark their invaluable website, www.winstonchurchill.org.

INDEX

195

ABOUT THE AUTHOR

STEVEN F. HAYWARD is a recognized authority on both Ronald Reagan and Winston Churchill, having written *The Age of Reagan: The Fall of the Old Liberal Order, 1964–1980* and *Churchill on Leadership*. A Ph.D. in American Studies, he is F. K. Weyerhaeuser Fellow at the American Enterprise Institute and Senior Fellow a the Pacific Research Institute. He writes frequently for *National Review, Reason,* and *Policy Review,* and his articles have appeared in the *New York Times, Wall Street Journal, Chicago Tribune, San Francisco Chronicle,* and *Baltimore Sun,* among many other newspapers. Hayward is currently at work on *The Age of Reagan: Lion at the Gate, 1980–1989,* to be published by Crown Forum in 2006.

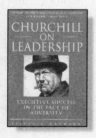